THE THIRTEEN COLONIES

Virginia

CRAIG A. DOHERTY

KATHERINE M. DOHERTY

Facts On File, Inc.

Note on Photos: Many of the illustrations and photographs used in this book are old, historical images. The quality of the prints is not always up to current standards, as in some cases the originals are from old or poor-quality negatives or are damaged. The content of the illustrations, however, made their inclusion important despite problems in reproduction.

Virginia

Copyright © 2005 by Craig A. Doherty and Katherine M. Doherty

Maps and graph copyright © 2005 by Facts On File, Inc.
Captions copyright © 2005 by Facts On File, Inc.

Facts On File, Inc.
132 West 31st Street
New York NY 10001

Library of Congress Cataloging-in-Publication Data

Doherty, Craig A.
    Virginia / Craig A. Doherty and Katherine M. Doherty.
       p. cm. — (The Thirteen colonies)
    Includes bibliographical references and index.
    ISBN 0-8160-5416-9
    1. Virginia—History—Colonial period, ca. 1600–1775—Juvenile literature. 2. Virginia—History—1775–1865—Juvenile literature. I. Doherty, Katherine M. II. Title.

    F229.D64 2005
    975.5'02—dc22   2004021004

Facts On File books are available at special discounts when purchased in bulk quantities for businesses, associations, institutions, or sales promotions. Please call our Special Sales Department in New York at (212) 967-8800 or (800) 322-8755.

You can find Facts On File on the World Wide Web at http://www.factsonfile.com.

Text design by Erika K. Arroyo
Cover design by Semadar Megged
Maps and graph by Sholto Ainslie

Printed in the United States of America

VB FOF 10 9 8 7 6 5 4 3 2 1

This book is printed on acid-free paper.

Contents

Introduction

In the 11th century, Vikings from Scandinavia sailed to North America. They explored the Atlantic coast and set up a few small settlements. In Newfoundland and Nova Scotia, Canada, archaeologists have found traces of these settlements. No one knows for sure why they did not establish permanent colonies. It may have been that it was too far away from their homeland. At about the same time, many Scandinavians were involved with raiding and establishing settlements along the coasts of what are now Great Britain and France. This may have offered greater rewards than traveling all the way to North America.

When the western part of the Roman Empire fell in 476, Europe lapsed into a period of almost 1,000 years of war, plague, and hardship. This period of European history is often referred to as the Dark Ages or Middle Ages. Communication between the different parts of Europe was almost nonexistent. If other Europeans knew about the Vikings' explorations westward, they left no record of it. Between the time of Viking exploration and Christopher Columbus's 1492 journey, Europe underwent many changes.

By the 15th century, Europe had experienced many advances. Trade within the area and with the Far East had created prosperity for the governments and many wealthy people. The Catholic Church had become a rich and powerful institution. Although wars would be fought and governments would come and go, the countries of Western Europe had become fairly strong. During this time, Europe rediscovered many of the arts and sciences that had

Vikings explored the Atlantic coast of North America in ships similar to this one. *(National Archives of Canada)*

existed before the fall of Rome. They also learned much from their trade with the Near and Far East. Historians refer to this time as the Renaissance, which means "rebirth."

At this time, some members of the Catholic Church did not like the direction the church was going. People such as Martin Luther and John Calvin spoke out against the church. They soon gained a number of followers who decided that they would protest and form their own churches. The members of these new churches were called Protestants. The movement to establish these new churches is called the Protestant Reformation. It would have a big impact on America as many Protestant groups would leave Europe so they could worship the way they wanted to.

In addition to religious dissent, problems arose with the overland trade routes to the Far East. The Ottoman Turks took control of the lands in the Middle East and disrupted trade. It was at this time that European explorers began trying to find a water route to the Far East. The explorers first sailed around Africa. Then an Italian named Christopher Columbus convinced the king and queen of Spain that it would be shorter to sail west to Asia rather than go around Africa. Most sailors and educated people at the time knew the world was round. However, Columbus made two errors in his calculations. First, he did not realize just how big the Earth is, and second, he did not know that the continents of North and South America blocked a westward route to Asia.

When Columbus made landfall in 1492, he believed that he was in the Indies, as the Far East was called at the time. For a period of time after Columbus, the Spanish controlled the seas and the exploration of what was called the New World. England tried to compete with the Spanish on the high seas, but their ships were no match for the floating fortresses of the Spanish Armada. These heavy ships, known as galleons, ruled the Atlantic.

In 1588, that all changed. A fleet of English ships fought a series of battles in which their smaller but faster and more maneuverable ships finally defeated the Spanish Armada. This opened up the New World to anyone willing to cross the ocean. Portugal, Holland, France, and England all funded voyages of exploration to the New World. In North America, the French explored the far north. The Spanish had already established colonies in what are now Florida, most of the Caribbean, and much of Central and South America. The

Depicted in this painting, Christopher Columbus completed three additional voyages to the Americas after his initial trip in search of a westward route to Asia in 1492. *(Library of Congress, Prints and Photographs Division [LC-USZ62-103980])*

Dutch bought Manhattan and would establish what would become New York, as well as various islands in the Caribbean and lands in South America. The English claimed most of the east coast of North America and set about creating colonies in a variety of ways.

Companies were formed in England and given royal charters to set up colonies. Some of the companies sent out military and trade expeditions to find gold and other riches. They employed men such as John Smith, Bartholomew Gosnold, and others to explore the lands they had been granted. Other companies found groups of Protestants who wanted to leave England and worked out deals that let them establish colonies. No matter what circumstances a colony was established under, the first settlers suffered hardships as

After Columbus's exploration of the Americas, the Spanish controlled the seas, largely because of their galleons, or large, heavy ships, that looked much like this model. *(Library of Congress, Prints and Photographs Division [LC-USZ62-103297])*

Virginia

they tried to build communities in what to them was a wilderness. They also had to deal with the people who were already there.

Native Americans lived in every corner of the Americas. There were vast and complex civilizations in Central and South America. The city that is now known as Cahokia was located along the Mississippi River in what is today Illinois and may have had as many as 50,000 residents. The people of Cahokia built huge earthen mounds that can still be seen today. There has been a lot of speculation as to the total population of Native Americans in 1492. Some have put the number as high as 40 million people.

Most of the early explorers encountered Native Americans. They often wrote descriptions of them for the people of Europe. They also kidnapped a few of these people, took them back to Europe, and put them on display. Despite the number of Native Americans, the Europeans still claimed the land as their own. The rulers of Europe and the Catholic Church at the time felt they had a right to take any lands they wanted from people who did not share their level of technology and who were not Christians.

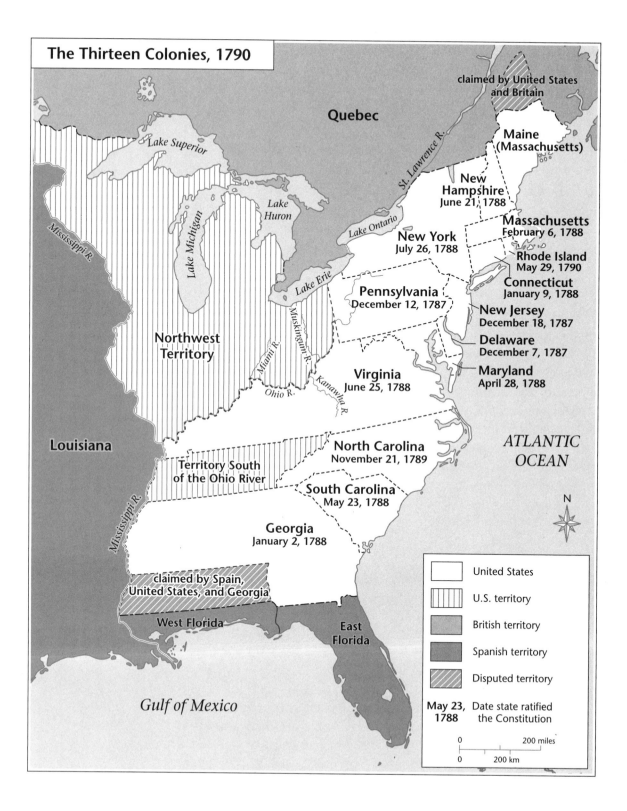

The Thirteen Colonies, 1790

claimed by United States and Britain

Quebec

Lake Superior

Lake Huron

Lake Michigan

Lake Ontario

Lake Erie

Mississippi R.

Maine (Massachusetts)

New Hampshire
June 21, 1788

New York
July 26, 1788

Massachusetts
February 6, 1788

Rhode Island
May 29, 1790

Connecticut
January 9, 1788

Pennsylvania
December 12, 1787

New Jersey
December 18, 1787

Delaware
December 7, 1787

Maryland
April 28, 1788

St. Lawrence R.

Northwest Territory

Miami R.

Muskingum R.

Ohio R.

Kanawha R.

Virginia
June 25, 1788

Louisiana

Territory South of the Ohio River

North Carolina
November 21, 1789

ATLANTIC OCEAN

South Carolina
May 23, 1788

Georgia
January 2, 1788

Mississippi R.

claimed by Spain, United States, and Georgia

West Florida

East Florida

Gulf of Mexico

N

United States

U.S. territory

British territory

Spanish territory

Disputed territory

May 23, 1788   Date state ratified the Constitution

0   200 miles

0   200 km

First Contacts

The coast of North America that became the colony of Virginia was seen by a number of European explorers in the years between the voyage of Christopher Columbus in 1492 and the arrival of the first English settlers in 1607. The French, Spanish, Dutch, and English all sent explorers and eventually colonists to North America. Overlapping and conflicting claims were made for much of the continent with little or no regard for the people who already inhabited the land.

Based on Columbus's voyages and the Spanish explorers and colonists who followed him, Spain laid claim to most of the Americas without even knowing the extent of what was claimed. In 1497, John Cabot sailed west for the English and explored the coast of North America from Labrador south to about latitude 38° north. This would have taken Cabot south to the vicinity of what is now the border between Virginia and Maryland on the Eastern Shore of Chesapeake Bay. Although it would be almost 100 years before the English attempted to set up a colony in what would become the thirteen colonies, they used Cabot's voyage to claim much of North America.

A French-sponsored voyage of exploration led by the Italian Giovanni da Verrazano in 1525 gave the French a claim to the east coast of North America. Despite these early claims, there was little interest in establishing colonies in what would become Virginia. The Spanish had discovered the wealth of the Aztec and

Inca and were growing rich off the plunder of Central and South America. For the English, most of the 16th century was a time of turmoil at home that left little time or resources for further exploration or to attempt colonizing what had already been claimed.

The Spanish established St. Augustine, Florida, in 1565. It is today the oldest continuously inhabited European community in North America. From there, the Spanish tried to establish a series of settlements up the coast in what is now Georgia, North Carolina, South Carolina, and Virginia. Some of these settlements were forts intended to help protect the Spanish treasure ships that sailed up the southern coast of North America following the favorable currents and winds of the Gulf Stream before turning east for Spain. The Spanish were also intent on converting as many of the original occupants of the Americas to Catholicism as possible and set up a number of missions to do so. In 1570, the Spanish started

Giovanni da Verrazano sailed to America in 1524 in search of a passageway to China. *(National Archives of Canada)*

a mission near what is today Fredericksburg, Virginia. Although this was the first European settlement in what was to become Virginia, it was quickly destroyed by Native Americans, leaving the area once again open to claim by whichever Europeans could establish and hang onto a colony there.

Sir Walter Raleigh, an Englishman who was a favorite of Queen Elizabeth I, was behind the first English attempt to colonize the area. It was Raleigh who named the place Virginia in honor of Elizabeth, who was known as the "virgin queen" because she never married or had children. Raleigh's colony at Roanoke Island, which is in what became North Carolina, was established in 1585. In the early years of the colony, war between England and Spain made it impossible for the English to send any supplies to the colony for almost five years. When ships arrived at Roanoke after the English had defeated the Spanish Armada in 1590, all the colonists had disappeared. It is now believed that the colonists who had not perished from disease or starvation had left Roanoke and moved north to what is now the Elizabeth River in Virginia, where they may have joined the Chesapeake Indians. The ancestors of the Chesapeake and the other Indians in what is now Virginia had been there for thousands of years and had a lifestyle well suited to the land and climate of the area.

THE NATIVE AMERICANS OF VIRGINIA

More than 11,000 years ago, at the end of the last ice age, the first Native Americans arrived in the area that is now Virginia. These first American Indians survived by hunting and gathering wild plants. They hunted large animals such as the wooly mammoth and the giant bison, as well as smaller animals, with stonetipped spears. Their stone tools and the bones of the animals they ate are about the only artifacts that archaeologists

After Elizabeth I granted Sir Walter Raleigh a charter, Raleigh repeatedly attempted to establish a colony in North America. *(Library of Congress, Prints and Photographs Division [LC-USZ6-670])*

have found. Between these first arrivals and the coming of Europeans, the lifestyles of the Indians of the area evolved into a complex society based on agriculture, hunting, and fishing.

It is estimated that there were more than 500 different Native American tribes in North America when the Europeans began to arrive. They spoke languages that have been broken down into approximately 50 different language families. The Native Americans of Virginia can be divided by the languages they spoke. The tribes along the coastal plain spoke versions of Algonquian languages. Heading west, the Piedmont was populated by a number of tribes that spoke Iroquoian languages. Farther west, in the mountains and western valley lived people who spoke languages from the Siouan family. Within each language group were a number of separate tribes. Some of these tribes, such as the Powhatan, Susquehanna, Tuscarora, and Cherokee, would have an impact on English settlement of the area. Other smaller tribes disappeared or were absorbed by larger tribes as conflicts and disease decimated the Native American population of Virginia.

There is no way to know how many Native Americans lived in what would become Virginia. However, a number of estimates have been made by modern scholars that suggest there may have been between 150,000 and 200,000 people living in Virginia in the 16th century. Although no one is sure how many people were in Virginia, the historical and archaeological record gives a fairly accurate picture of how they lived.

Despite their tribal and language differences, the Native Americans of Virginia all lived a similar lifestyle. Scientists refer to their way of living as Woodland Culture. This is due to the fact that many of their needs were supplied by the extensive forests that covered eastern North America at the time. Food, clothing, and the materials to make their houses and many of their tools and utensils came

When English colonists settled on Roanoke Island, coastal Algonquians now known as the Roanoke lived there. John White, an artist who participated in an effort to colonize the island in 1584, created the image of a Roanoke chief that is the basis for this engraving by Theodor de Bry. *(Library of Congress, Prints and Photographs Division [LC-USZ62-89909])*

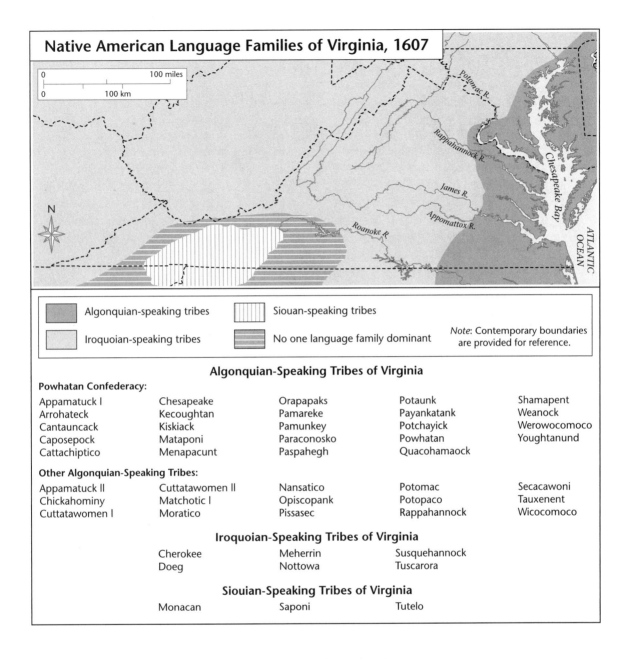

Native American Language Families of Virginia, 1607

0   100 miles

0   100 km

N

Potomac R.

Rappahannock R.

James R.

Appomattox R.

Roanoke R.

Chesapeake Bay

ATLANTIC OCEAN

Algonquian-speaking tribes   Siouan-speaking tribes

Iroquoian-speaking tribes   No one language family dominant

Note: Contemporary boundaries are provided for reference.

Algonquian-Speaking Tribes of Virginia

Powhatan Confederacy:

Appamatuck I	Chesapeake	Orapapaks	Potaunk	Shamapent
Arrohateck	Kecoughtan	Pamareke	Payankatank	Weanock
Cantauncack	Kiskiack	Pamunkey	Potchayick	Werowocomoco
Caposepock	Mataponi	Paraconosko	Powhatan	Youghtanund
Cattachiptico	Menapacunt	Paspahegh	Quacohamaock	

Other Algonquian-Speaking Tribes:

Appamatuck II	Cuttatawomen II	Nansatico	Potomac	Secacawoni
Chickahominy	Matchotic I	Opiscopank	Potopaco	Tauxenent
Cuttatawomen I	Moratico	Pissasec	Rappahannock	Wicocomoco

Iroquoian-Speaking Tribes of Virginia

Cherokee	Meherrin	Susquehannock
Doeg	Nottowa	Tuscarora

Siouian-Speaking Tribes of Virginia

Monacan	Saponi	Tutelo

from the forest. They were also accomplished farmers who grew corn, beans, and squash to eat, as well as tobacco, which they smoked during social and ceremonial occasions. The cultivation of tobacco would become the main source of wealth for the English colonists in Virginia.

Corn

Corn was first cultivated 7,000 years ago by Native Americans living in what is now Mexico. Over time, through careful seed selection and hybridization, Native Americans were able to develop from a type of wild grass more than 700 varieties of corn. Different varieties were needed for different purposes and growing conditions. The transition from hunting and gathering to an agriculture-based lifestyle allowed Native Americans to settle down in one area and for their populations to grow.

There are five main types of corn. Popcorn was probably the earliest type that was developed. Its small kernels open when they are heated. Flint corn is similar to popcorn but with bigger kernels and was adapted to grow in northern climates. Flour corn is a variety that can be ground into cornmeal and used to make tortillas or cornbread. Dent corn is a variety that can be both ground into meal or used whole in soups and stews. Sweet corn is the type of corn that is usually eaten fresh as corn on the cob. The Native Americans in Virginia grew all of these types of corn.

As farmers, Native Americans excelled. They had discovered that their three main crops—corn, beans, and squash—could be grown together. The corn was planted in small hills with several cornstalks planted in each hill. Beans were planted in the hills as well. The bean vines used the corn stalks for support. Beans are a legume, which means that they have the ability to add nitrogen to the soil as they grow. Corn needs lots of nitrogen. So the two plants helped each other. The squash was planted in the spaces between the corn and bean hills. The large leaves of the squash plants shaded out many of the weeds, making it easier for the women of the tribe who were responsible for tending the fields.

After a few years of use, fields would begin to lose their fertility. Then new fields would be cleared. Without modern equipment, land clearing presented a challenge for Native Americans. Over time, they had learned how to use fire in a number of ways to help them manage the land. To clear a field, they would girdle the trees (cut away the bark in a line all the way around the tree), which killed them. When the trees died, the area would be burned and then used as a new field. They also used fire in other ways. Often

Deer Hunting

Deer hunting was an important activity for the Native Americans of Virginia. Many groups considered the killing of a deer one of the indications that a boy had reached manhood. It was also an activity that was carried on in a variety of ways. One hunter working alone was the hardest way to hunt a deer. The hunter would use his knowledge of his quarry and his ability to sneak through the woods to get close enough to the deer to kill it with his bow. At other times, a group would work together to drive deer through the woods toward other hunters who were hidden.

The largest hunts might involve most of the residents of a village. They would build a large funnel-shaped fence and then would often use fire to drive the deer into the wide end of the funnel. At the narrow end, there would be a pen where waiting hunters would slaughter the deer with spears and even knives. In the first years of the Jamestown Colony, the colonists often had to trade with members of the Powhatan Confederacy to get deer meat. Few of the early settlers had the skills necessary to hunt for their own meat.

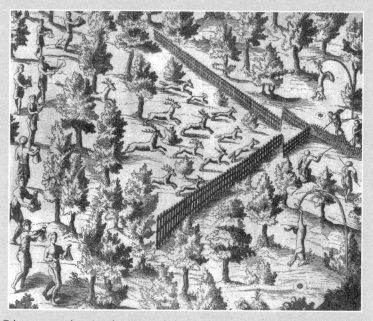

In this early 17th-century drawing by Samuel de Champlain, an American Indian deer hunt is in progress. Some American Indians startle the deer into running toward traps depicted on the right side of the image. *(National Library of Canada)*

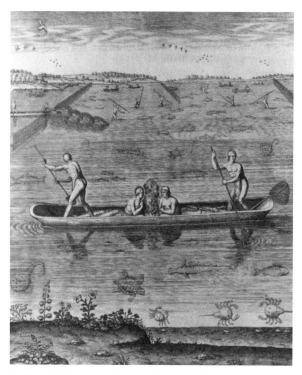

In this 1590s engraving by Theodor de Bry, American Indians along the east coast of the United States fish and prepare traps. *(Library of Congress, Prints and Photographs Division [LC-USZ62-576])*

the woods were burned to keep down the brushy plants that grew under the forest canopy. This practice made it easier to travel in the woods and also encouraged the growth of useful plants. It also created better habitat for the native deer and turkeys that were staples in the diet of Woodland Indians.

Among the many birds and animals that the Native Americans of Virginia hunted, the deer was the most important. Every part of the deer was utilized. The meat was roasted fresh or dried for later use. The hide was tanned and was the most important source of material for clothing and moccasins. Bones and antlers were fashioned into a variety of tools that included drills, fishhooks, scrapers, and many other useful items. The sinew, the fibrous covering on muscles, was used like string to attach stone points to spears and arrows, as bow strings, and many other applications that might require string.

Those tribes that lived along the Tidewater also harvested a wide variety of fish and shellfish. At the time, the bays and estuaries of what is now Virginia had many more fish and shellfish than they do today. Fish were so plentiful that people were able to use a rope with a loop in it to lasso large sturgeon that swam up the rivers. They also used hooks, nets, traps, and spears to catch fish. Even those tribes that lived inland took advantage of the fish that were plentiful in the lakes, rivers, and streams of their territories.

During spring spawning runs, the Native Americans of Virginia might leave their home villages and travel to locations that provided good opportunities to fish. In the fall, they might travel to a temporary hunting camp. Sometimes different tribes fought over hunting territory, especially the Algonquian-speaking tribes and those of the Piedmont who spoke Iroquoian languages. Most of the year, however, the Native Americans of Virginia lived in permanent villages that were usually located along the banks of the area's streams and rivers. Their fields were nearby.

Native American villages ranged in size from fewer than 50 people to more than 1,000. Often the villages were surrounded by a palisade. This was a high fence made of pointed logs. The palisade gave the village protection from raids by enemies. Within the palisade were houses. The Native Americans of Virginia, like others of the Woodland Culture, built two primary types of houses—wigwams and longhouses. Wigwams were circular. Longhouses, as their name suggests, were long and rectangular.

Both styles of houses were built in a similar way. Saplings (young, flexible trees) were cut down, and their larger ends were stuck into the ground. For a wigwam, the saplings were arranged in a circle and then bent into the center, where they were tied together to form a dome. For a longhouse, the saplings were

To protect themselves, some tribes built palisades (also called stockades), or a perimeter around their villages made of tall timbers, sharpened at one end and driven into the ground. *(Library of Congress)*

arranged in two parallel rows 12 to 25 feet apart and from 30 to more than 100 feet long. The saplings were bent into the center to form an arch. Both types of houses were covered with bark, and a hole was left in the center for the smoke of winter cooking fires to escape. In the warm months, the cooking would be done outside.

Inside these houses were raised platforms that were used for sitting and workspace during the day and as beds at night. Longhouses were usually divided into sections that were home to one or two nuclear families of parents and their children. All the families that lived in one longhouse were usually part of one large extended family. The family was the most important social unit in Woodland Culture and often worked collectively to take care of the needs of the whole family. Next in importance was the village in which the family lived. After the welfare of the family and the village was assured, people turned their attention to their tribal affiliations.

Prior to the 17th century, there is little evidence to suggest that there were any complex tribal alliances. However, shortly before the settlement of Jamestown in 1607 by the English, the leader of the Powhatan Wahunsonakok, whom the English referred to simply as Powhatan, created a confederacy of more than 26 tribes and bands of Algonquian-speaking peoples. Some of these groups joined the confederacy willingly, while others were forced to join after being attacked by Powhatan's warriors. Some historians have suggested that Powhatan was reacting to the early contacts with Europeans in the area, but this is hard to prove. There are no written records prior to the coming of the English in 1607, and the early accounts from Jamestown by Captain John Smith and others were often intended to attract new colonists. They tended to be more like advertising than an accurate historical account.

It was Powhatan who for a variety of reasons eventually helped the English at Jamestown. Without Native Americans to provide them with food and teach them how to survive in the New World, the colony at Jamestown might very well have ended up like the Lost Colony of Roanoke. By the time Powhatan's brother Opechancanough took the leadership of the confederacy in 1622, there were many more English to defeat. With Opechancanough's leadership, the Powhatan Confederacy lost a series of wars against the

In this detail from a 1624 map by John Smith, Wahunsonakok, whom the English referred to as Powhatan, meets with his people, the Powhatan. *(Library of Congress)*

colonists, and through warfare and disease were almost completely wiped out.

European diseases played a terrible role in the defeat of the Native Americans of Virginia and the rest of North America. Native Americans had no resistance to European diseases such as measles and mumps. However, the disease that took the greatest toll in Native Americans was smallpox, which also affected Europeans.

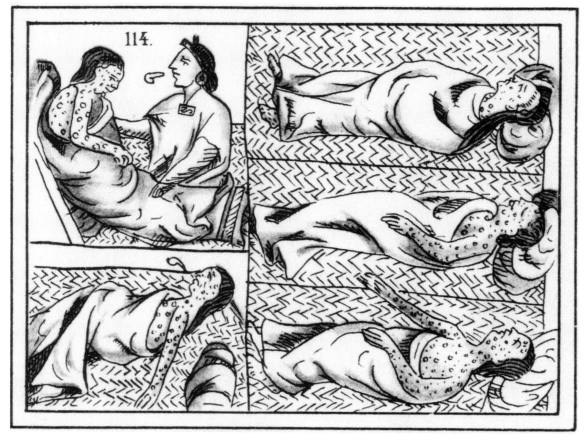

Published in *Historia de las cosas de Nueva España* in the 1570s, this illustration shows Aztec people sick with smallpox. American Indians suffered great losses from the influx of European diseases that accompanied colonization. *(Library of Congress)*

For Native Americans, smallpox was almost always fatal. Some scientists estimate that between 90 and 95 percent of the Native American population eventually died of European diseases. Between disease and warfare, the Native Americans of Virginia and other colonies continually lost territory to wave after wave of new arrivals from Europe.

2

First Settlements
in Virginia

After the failed attempts to establish the Roanoke colony in the 1580s, it took more than 20 years and a new king in England before the next colony in the area was attempted. In 1603, Queen Elizabeth I died without an heir to the throne of England. James, whose mother, Mary, queen of Scots, was Elizabeth's cousin, became James I, king of England and Scotland. Under James I's leadership, companies were formed and granted charters to establish colonies in North America.

The first two companies formed to establish colonies in North America were made up of investors from two of England's major cities. One company was known as the Virginia Company of Plymouth. It sponsored the colony of Puritans who arrived at what became Plymouth, Massachusetts, in 1620. The other company was known as the Virginia Company of London (often referred to as the London Company). It sponsored the first permanent English settlement in what would become the United States at Jamestown,

While Elizabeth I ruled England and Ireland, she supported exploration and colonization efforts and the strengthening of the navy. *(Library of Congress, Prints and Photographs Division [LC-USZ62-120887])*

Virginia, in 1607. The first settlement and the river it was situated on were both named for King James I.

The charter that James I gave to the London Company in 1606 defined their grant as extending from latitude 34° to 45° north and

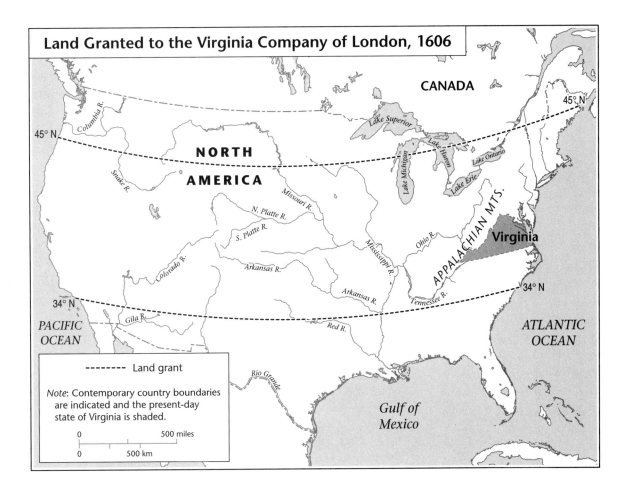

Land Granted to the Virginia Company of London, 1606

CANADA

45° N

NORTH

AMERICA

45° N

Columbia R.

Snake R.

Lake Superior

Lake Michigan

Lake Huron

Lake Ontario

Lake Erie

N. Platte R.

S. Platte R.

Missouri R.

Ohio R.

APPALACHIAN MTS.

Virginia

Colorado R.

Arkansas R.

Mississippi R.

34° N

34° N

PACIFIC
OCEAN

Gila R.

Arkansas R.

Tennessee R.

Red R.

ATLANTIC
OCEAN

- - - - - - - Land grant

Note: Contemporary country boundaries
are indicated and the present-day
state of Virginia is shaded.

0   500 miles

0   500 km

Rio Grande

*Gulf of
Mexico*

from the Atlantic Ocean west to the Pacific Ocean. This gave the London Company rights to all the land from approximately where the border of North and South Carolina meets the Atlantic Ocean north to the point where the border between Maine and New Brunswick meets the Atlantic. This grant included a huge portion of what is today the United States as well as some of southern Ontario, Canada.

The London Company lasted only until 1622. Much of the land it was originally granted was later given away in other grants by James I and his descendants. During the 16 years that the London Company existed, much effort and many resources were put into the Jamestown Colony by the company in hopes of turning a profit. No profits were ever realized, but the colony grew into the largest in America and played an important role in the creation of the United States.

JAMESTOWN

On December 19, 1606, three ships—the *Susan Constant*, the *Godspeed*, and the *Discovery*—left England headed for Virginia. The ships carried supplies and 104 men who were to establish a colony in Virginia. Many of the men who had volunteered to go to Virginia were unsuited for the task. They were adventurers and the younger sons of the nobility who were interested only in a chance to find wealth as the Spanish had done in Central and South America. At the time in England, only the oldest son was allowed to inherit the wealth of his father. Many of the younger sons joined the military or sought out schemes like the Virginia Colony that might provide them with the type of lifestyle they had experienced on the estates of their fathers.

Very few of these men expected to have to work for their survival. For that, a number of indentured servants had been recruited for the first trip to Virginia. These were men who had no resources

Indentured Servants

The original leaders of the efforts to colonize North America intended to use the structured society of England as their model. They foresaw a landed nobility served by a working class. The question was how to get people willing to be laborers and servants to agree to go to the colonies. The Virginia Company of London probably did not invent the idea; however, they definitely put to use the idea of indentured servants.

Those who went to Virginia as indentured servants signed an agreement to work for the company for a term of seven years. In exchange for their labor, they would receive transportation to the colony; food, clothing, and shelter; and free land at the end of their indenture. Some have esti-

mated that during the 17th and 18th century between one-half and two-thirds of all people who came to the English colonies in North America arrived as indentured servants.

The terms of indenture that were signed between the company and an individual were transferable. Often ship captains held the indenture papers and would sell them upon arrival in the colonies. In the 17th century, as tobacco plantations grew in size and wealth, it was by the labor of indentured servants that many were able to succeed as planters. As time went on, the planters of Virginia, Maryland, and the Carolinas found a cheaper source of labor: slaves from Africa, who replaced the indentured servants.

Captain John Smith helped found Jamestown in present-day Virginia.
(National Archives of Canada)

who agreed to work for the company for seven years in exchange for their passage and land at the end of their indenture. The indentured servants did what little work was accomplished in the beginnings of the colony.

The time it took to sail from England to North America varied greatly depending on the weather. For the three ships of the

Captain John Smith
(1580–1631)

John Smith was born into a farming family in Willoughby, Lincolnshire, England. He rose in status in English society through his exploits as a soldier. He first volunteered to fight against the Spanish on the European continent. After that he spent some time as a sailor on a merchant ship in the Mediterranean. Then, in 1600, he joined the Austrian army in its war against the Ottoman Turks in Hungary. Smith was rewarded for his bravery and leadership by Prince Bathori of Transylvania, whose homeland was the site of much of the fighting.

During one battle in Transylvania, Smith was captured by the Turks and taken to Istanbul, where he was sold as a slave. Smith

John Smith's descriptions of the colonies generated much interest in them. This particular map of Virginia was published in one of Smith's books about his explorations. *(Library of Congress, Prints and Photographs Division [LC-USZ62-116706])*

was able to escape to Russia by killing the brother of the noblewoman who had bought him. For the next few years Smith traveled around eastern Europe and North Africa before returning to England in 1605. Back in England, he signed on to take part in a colony in Guiana in South America, but that enterprise never got going. It was at that point that Smith joined the Virginia Company of London to help in the establishment of a colony in North America. He played a critical role in keeping the struggling colony going.

After returning to England in 1609, Smith spent much of the rest of his life writing about his exploits in Virginia and elsewhere. His *A Map of Virginia* (1612) and *A Description of New England* (1616) did much to excite people in England about colonizing North America. Many have come to realize that, although Captain Smith was an excellent storyteller, he frequently distorted the facts to make himself look good, his experiences more exciting, and North America more appealing.

London Company, the crossing took more than four months. During the long voyage, some of the problems that the colony would experience were foreshadowed by dissension among the expedition's leaders. Most of the leaders were members of England's upper class and had no real experience that suited them for building a colony. However, there was one man who had the respect of the company because of his accomplishments as a soldier and adventurer. This man was Captain John Smith. Before the ships reached their first stop in the Canary Islands, Smith had shown his lack of respect for those who considered themselves his social superiors. To silence him, his main opponent, Edward Maria Wingfield, charged him with trying to start a mutiny and locked him up until they reached Virginia.

The three ships arrived at Chesapeake Bay on April 26, 1607. Everyone was eager to go ashore, but the captain of the *Susan Constant*, Christopher Newport, was in charge until they had selected a site for their colony. Newport wanted to do some exploring before he let everyone go ashore. He took a party of 30 men, made up mostly of sailors and soldiers, and went exploring. They took the ship's longboat and went ashore on the south side of the bay. They spent the day looking around without incident and were impressed with the land they found.

However, as darkness fell and the men were making their way back to their boat, they were attacked by a small group of Indians. Two of the English party were wounded. Considering the unprovoked attack, a location that could be defended became a primary concern for the small group of colonists. They had brought a small sloop, called a shallop, along with them and, once it was rigged and launched, it was used to explore the bay. During the trips around the bay, a number of places were given names. The two capes at the mouth of the bay were named for the king's two sons: Cape Henry on the south side and Cape Charles on the north.

Now that they were in Virginia, it was time for the colonists to open the sealed box that had been given to them by the directors of the company. Inside the box was a list of names of the men who were to run the colony as the resident council. The seven names on the list were: Christopher Newport, Bartholomew Gosnold, and John Martin, who were the captains of the three ships; Edward Wingfield, John Ratcliffe, and George Kendall, who were influential members of the group; and the one name that surprised the other six, John Smith. Later, on May 13, Wingfield was elected president or governor by the council and would find himself once again at odds with Smith.

The rivers of Virginia are navigable well inland to what is known as the fall line—the place of the first rapids or waterfall on a river. The colonists explored far up what they named the James River looking for a site to start their colony. A scouting party in the shallop went first, followed by the three ships. On May 12, George Percy reported back to Newport that he had found a good spot. On May 13, 1607, the fleet arrived off a peninsula that stuck out into the river. It was a peninsula connected to the main bank of the river only by a narrow piece of land. They were almost 60 miles up the James River and decided this would be the spot for Jamestown.

The site could be easily defended and was far enough upriver so that it was unlikely they would be bothered by the Spanish. However, there were a number of problems with the site. First, there was no freshwater on the peninsula. Although the land close to the river was suitable for building, much of the peninsula was marshy. Despite the fact that they were far from the ocean, the water in the river was brackish. It was a mixture of saltwater and freshwater that was unsuitable for drinking. Also, much of the low-lying land around Jamestown was swampy and the perfect environment for breeding clouds of disease-carrying mosquitoes.

The site was not the only problem faced by the first settlers at Jamestown. Soon a number of the colonists were sick. Malaria from the mosquitoes, dysentery from drinking bad water, and other ailments caused many to be unable to help build the colony. Although the late-spring weather was pleasant when the colonists arrived, they were soon confronted by the summer heat. England has a relatively cool climate, and the colonists found it hard to adjust to the heat of a Virginia summer. Many of the upper-class colonists had no

These architectural remains are from a building believed to have been built in 1624 as part of the Jamestown settlement in present-day Virginia. *(Library of Congress, Prints and Photographs Division [HABS, VA, 48-JAM, 4-3])*

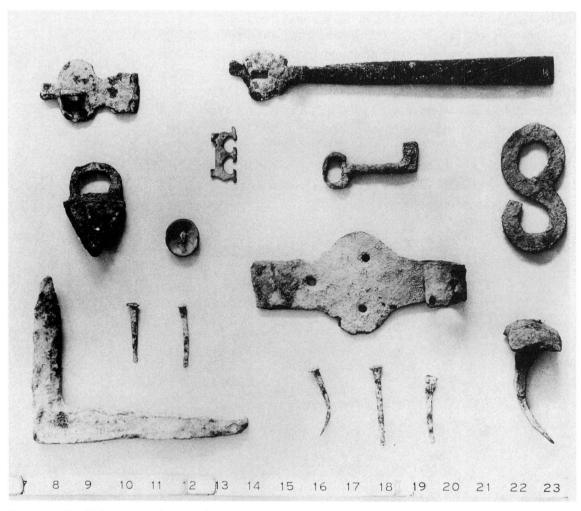

Shown in this 20th-century photograph are some tools excavated from a site in Jamestown. *(Library of Congress, Prints and Photographs Division [HABS, VA, 48-JAM, 4-4])*

intention or the ability to do physical labor. Many who were well enough spent their time gambling and complaining.

In addition to all those problems, the colony was extremely short of food. They had planned to arrive in time to plant crops, but the length of their crossing and the time that it took to select a site prevented them from getting a crop in the ground for the first growing season. At the end of June, Newport headed back to England for more supplies. By midsummer, the colonists' supplies of beef, biscuits, and cheese had been used up. All they had left was barley and wheat that was infested with worms. Although there was plentiful game in the woods and fish in the river, none of the colonists really knew how to hunt or fish. It was not long before the colonists began dying.

According to John Smith's accounts, he and some colonists were taken prisoner by the Powhatan Indians in December 1607. This image shows the Powhatan celebrating their capture of them. *(Library of Congress, Prints and Photographs Division [LC-USZ62-31735])*

Wingfield was blamed for many of the problems and was replaced as president by John Ratcliffe. Smith would later write that during the first summer ". . . the living were scarce able to bury the dead." By September, half of the colonists had died. Even more would have died had not John Smith stepped up and begun trading with the local Indians. Ratcliffe appointed Smith supply master, and he would go out with mirrors, beads, tools, and trinkets and return with corn and venison (deer meat). It was on one of these trading expeditions that one of the most famous incidents in the chronicles written by Captain Smith is alleged to have occurred.

In this late 19th-century print, Matooka, more often known as Pocahontas, saves Captain John Smith's life, a story told by Smith that anthropologists have found evidence to disprove. *(Library of Congress, Prints and Photographs Division [LC-UAZ62-5254])*

Pocahontas
(ca. 1595–1617)

Pocahontas's contact with the Jamestown colony was well documented. However, her role as John Smith's savior is questioned by many. What is known is that Pocahontas was frequently in Jamestown as an emissary from her father and helped the English settlers in many ways.

In 1613, during a time of fighting between the Powhatan and the English, Pocahontas was captured by Samuel Argall, who had assumed the leadership of Jamestown when Smith had gone back to England. During the year that Pocahontas was held at Jamestown, she learned to speak English and learned many English customs. She is also reported to have converted to Christianity and been baptized into the Anglican Church. At this time, Pocahontas was given the English name Rebecca.

On April 5, 1614, Pocahontas married John Rolfe, one of the colonists at Jamestown. Their marriage helped bring about a period of relative calm between the English and the Powhatan Confederacy. In 1615, Pocahontas and John Rolfe had a son named Thomas. When Thomas was two, his parents took him to England. When their ship left England to return to Virginia, Pocahontas became ill. The ship put in at Gravesend, England, and Pocahontas died on March 21, 1617. John Rolfe returned to Virginia to tell Powhatan of his daughter's death. Both died shortly thereafter. Thomas Rolfe stayed with relatives in England until 1640, when he returned to Virginia and became one of the colony's most successful tobacco growers.

Pocahontas's story has been told and retold many times, often embellished to make it even more exciting or romantic than it actually was. This mixture of fact and fiction has made her one of the most recognizable American Indian women in the history of the United States.

In late December 1607, Smith was on a trading trip along the Chickahominy River. He and the colonists with him were attacked by Powhatan Indians. Several of the colonists were killed, and Smith was captured. His captors brought him before Wahunsonakok (called Powhatan by the English) the chief of the Powhatan tribe and leader of the confederacy of tribes along the Virginia Tidewater, known as the Powhatan Confederacy. According to later embellishments to the story by Smith, he was brought before the chief and two flat stones were brought out. He was forced to put his head down on one of the stones while some of the warriors seemed ready to kill him.

As the warriors raised their clubs, the chief's 12-year-old daughter Matooka, who is more familiarly known as Pocahontas, supposedly came forward and pleaded that Smith's life be saved. For many years, historians accepted Smith's version of the story about Pocahontas saving his life. What anthropologists have more recently suggested is that the whole event was staged as part of an elaborate adoption ceremony in which Smith was made an honorary member of the Powhatan tribe. Whatever the true story is, from that point forward there were good relations between the Powhatan and the colonists, and Pocahontas often visited Jamestown.

Newport returned in January 1608, with supplies and 70 new settlers, including the colony's first two women. Again the company had recruited a number of gentlemen for the colony. This caused Smith to write back to England that he would rather they send "30 carpenters, husbandmen, gardeners, fisher men, blacksmiths, masons, and diggers up of trees' roots, well-provided, then a thousand of such as we have . . ." To make matters worse, only a week after supplies had arrived a fire broke out in the community, burning a number of buildings, including the storehouse that held all the colony's supplies.

Hunger and disease once again began to take their toll. By spring 1608, only 38 colonists were still alive. Smith had been elected governor in January 1608, and he ruled with a firm hand. He started a policy that required colonists, no matter their station back in England, to work if they expected to be fed. Under Smith's stern rule, the colony began to grow slowly. In September 1609, a third shipment of colonists and supplies arrived from England.

Unfortunately, Smith was badly wounded when his gunpowder exploded. He decided to return to England until his wounds healed. He would never return to Virginia, but when he left, the colony had a church, a new storehouse, a blockhouse for protection, many new houses, and more than 500 residents.

3

From Starving to Prosperity

THE STARVING TIME

In 1609, the members of the London Company took a hard look at their attempt to start a profitable colony. They were still somewhat optimistic but felt a number of changes were needed to ensure a profit for the investors. A new charter was written up and granted in 1609. Under the new charter, the organization of the company was simplified, and it was allowed to sell stock to the public. With the money raised from the sale of stock, a new plan was set in motion. Thomas West, 12th baron De La Warr, was appointed Virginia's governor. He arranged for supplies, 500 colonists, and a convoy of nine ships to head out to Virginia.

For most of the 500 colonists in Jamestown in the fall, the reorganization of the company came too late. The winter of 1609 to 1610 turned out to be even worse for Jamestown. Those who survived it called it the "starving time." Once again, disease ran through the colony, killing many. Without Smith to negotiate with the Indians, little help came to Jamestown from the surrounding tribes. Food shortages caused the greatest suffering.

Colonists are reported to have eaten all their animals, including their pets and any rodents or snakes they could find around the village. They also ate their leather shoes and clothing. As the situation worsened in the winter, some colonists even ate the bodies of the colonists who had died. The relief fleet headed by Lord De La Warr was delayed.

Thomas West, Lord De La Warr, brought three ships full of supplies to the Jamestown colony in early 1610, just as the colonists were preparing to abandon the colony. West was governor of Virginia for the next year. His name, *De La Warr,* was later used for the colony northeast of Virginia. *(Independence National Historical Park)*

Some of the ships left England with Sir Thomas Gates in charge. First, they spent weeks becalmed, stuck due to lack of wind, almost within sight of England. Then they were shipwrecked in the Bahamas and had to build two smaller ships out of the wreckage to get them to Virginia. When Gates arrived in Jamestown in May 1610, there were only 60 people remaining in the colony. Some had left to try and make it on their own and were never heard from again. However, more than 400 people had died during the "starving time."

Gates had 100 new colonists with him and supplies for everybody. He was also expecting Lord De La Warr to arrive shortly. However, the colonists who had survived the winter had had enough. They convinced Gates to take them to the English fishing colony in Newfoundland where they might find a large ship so they could sail back to England. Gates gave in and loaded the remaining colonists onto the two small ships that had been built in the Bahamas.

On June 10, 1610, they were about to sail out of Chesapeake Bay and head north to Newfoundland when they met up with Lord De La Warr. Gates turned around, and Jamestown was once again inhabited by colonists. Between the people who came with Gates and Lord De La Warr and the survivors of the "starving time," there were more than 300 people in Jamestown. Under the firm control of Lord De La Warr, many of the problems that faced Jamestown were corrected. By the time he headed back to England in 1611, the colony was starting to grow and new towns were being formed. Soon, the establishment of tobacco as a cash crop for the colony would ensure that Virginia would become the largest and one of the most prosperous of the 13 English colonies in North America.

TOBACCO GROWING

Although the colony of Virginia had survived the starving time and was beginning to slowly grow, the colonists had yet to find any way to make a profit for themselves or the company. In 1612, John Rolfe decided to experiment with growing tobacco in Virginia. He was a pipe smoker who had tried the locally grown Indian tobacco and had found it inferior to the Spanish tobacco that was grown in the Caribbean. Rolfe acquired tobacco seed from the Caribbean from a passing ship captain and made a number of experimental plantings over the course of two years.

In 1613, the first samples of Rolfe's tobacco were sent to England for evaluation. The English tobacco merchants were very impressed. They wanted all the tobacco that Rolfe could supply. In 1615, he shipped 20,000 pounds of tobacco. The Virginian tobacco boom had begun. Soon everyone was trying to grow

In this scene from an engraving published in 1800, a slave on a Virginia plantation cures tobacco leaves that have been harvested. *(Library of Congress, Prints and Photographs Division [LC-USZ62-72333])*

Tobacco

Tobacco is one of many plants cultivated by American Indians that had an impact on the rest of the world. Columbus brought the first tobacco to Europe after he had seen Indians smoking pipes they called "tobagos." It is from this word that the term *tobacco* came. The idea of smoking tobacco caught on in Spain and was soon exported throughout Europe. For more than 100 years, the Spanish had a monopoly on tobacco and supplied the growing demand.

Early advocates of tobacco use claimed that it had numerous health benefits. Modern medical science has long since proven that the nicotine in tobacco is an addictive substance and that tobacco use causes or contributes to numerous life-threatening diseases. Even so, tobacco growing continues to be a profitable business in Virginia and neighboring states. The large tobacco companies in the United States continue to meet the demand for cigarettes and other tobacco products.

In this scene from an engraving published in 1800, a slave on a Virginia plantation prepares tobacco leaves so that they may be aired in a large barn. *(Library of Congress, Prints and Photographs Division [LC-USZ62-72333])*

tobacco in any open ground they could find, including the streets of Jamestown. The directors of the company had mixed feelings about going into the tobacco growing business. However, changes

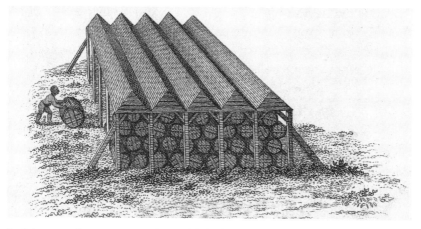

In this scene from an engraving published in 1800, a slave on a Virginia plantation rolls a barrel full of dried tobacco leaves into a storage area. *(Library of Congress, Prints and Photographs Division [LC-USZ62-72333])*

in the company's policies and serious financial problems combined to encourage tobacco growing.

To try and get more colonists, the company made a new offer. Those who would pay their own way to Virginia would be given 50 acres of land. Also, for each additional person's passage paid, they would receive another 50 acres. Because money could be made with land in Virginia, people began flocking to the colony.

In this scene from an engraving published in 1800, some people on a Virginia plantation examine cured tobacco leaves in a barn. *(Library of Congress, Prints and Photographs Division [LC-USZ62-72333])*

This was the beginning of the plantation system that would dominate Virginia throughout the colonial period and beyond. As people began to make money from tobacco, they used their profits to acquire more and more land as well as more laborers to work it.

PLANTATION ECONOMY

After John Rolfe married Pocahontas in 1614, there was a period of relative peace between the colonists and the tribes of the Powhatan Confederacy. This peaceful period and the desire to grow more tobacco gave many colonists the courage to move out of Jamestown and begin clearing land. The large number of navigable rivers and inlets that emptied into Chesapeake Bay provided a unique opportunity for the colonists. The oceangoing ships of the time could sail right up to the docks built by each tobacco farm.

As the Tidewater plantations grew in size, each became a direct trading partner with merchants in England. The company discouraged artisans and manufacturers from going to Virginia. In this way, most of the profits from tobacco were spent buying goods produced in England. Each tobacco grower had an account with a tobacco merchant. The merchant filled orders from the growers for tools, furniture, clothes, books, and other goods not available in the colony. These goods were charged against the planter's tobacco account and sent on the ship that was to pick up the tobacco.

Over time, as the land that had direct access to the ocean was taken up, many small farms were developed inland. Often these inland farmers had to depend on the nearest Tidewater plantation to serve as the shipping point for their tobacco. Many of these plantations became middlemen in the tobacco trade. Some even established stores where the small-scale farmers could buy needed goods. A division began to grow in Virginia between the wealthiest Tidewater planters and those who had small farms in the interior. This division continued well into the 19th century.

A YEAR OF FIRSTS: 1619

The success of the tobacco growers did not do enough to make the stockholders in the London Company happy. In 1618, one more attempt was made to revitalize the company and its colony. Even

As shown in this woodcut, slaves from Africa were first introduced to Jamestown in 1619. *(North Wind Picture Archives)*

more liberal land grants were offered, which encouraged the plantation system. A new governor, Sir George Yeardley, who had already spent time in Virginia, was selected. More new colonists were recruited. This time, however, a large contingent of single women was sent.

By 1619, there were almost 2,200 colonists in Virginia. Most of them were single men. To try and help these men, and make a profit as well, the company decided to recruit women to go to Virginia. Approximately 100 women were sent to Jamestown in 1619. The company provided their passage to the colony. Most of them quickly found husbands in Virginia. There was a catch, though. The new husband was responsible for paying the company back for his wife's passage. For each woman who married, the company collected 120 pounds of tobacco.

In 1619, another type of colonist also arrived in Virginia for the first time. A Dutch ship arrived in Jamestown in need of supplies. However, the only commodity they had to trade for the supplies was 20 African slaves. The Dutch were one of the major transporters of slaves from Africa to the Americas. The idea of using slaves instead of indentured servants caught on slowly in Virginia. By 1670, there were 2,000 blacks in Virginia, and most were held as slaves. By the middle of the 1700s there were more than 100,000 blacks in the colony, and they made up 44 percent of the population. Slavery would continue as a source of labor for the plantations of Virginia until the Civil War in the 1860s.

The arrival of a boatload of women and the first slaves were important events in the history of Virginia. However, another event

Slaves were integral to the survival of Virginia plantations. Slaves usually had separate housing, such as this wooden building built in the 1840s in the vicinity of Long Island, Virginia, and shown in a 1960 photograph. *(Library of Congress, Prints and Photographs Division [HABS, VA, 16-LONI.V, 1K-1])*

In this engraving of a painting, Patrick Henry speaks to the members of the House of Burgesses. *(National Archives, Still Picture Records, NWDNS-148-GW-872)*

that took place in 1619 had a great impact on what would become the United States. When Governor Yeardley left for Virginia, he had instructions to create a colonial assembly.

The colonized part of Virginia was divided into 11 political districts called boroughs. All the free adult male property owners were given the right to vote. Each borough elected two representatives who were known as burgesses. On July 30, 1619, 20 of the burgesses met in the church in Jamestown. It was the only building big enough to hold this first meeting of what was called the House of Burgesses. The heat of summer and the fact that a number of the burgesses became ill cut the first session short and little was accomplished.

However, the idea that the colonists should have some say in their own governing had been planted. The House of Burgesses set a precedent that would be followed to a lesser or greater degree in all the English colonies in North America. More than 150 years later, the seed planted in Virginia would turn into a full-blown revolution as the American colonists fought for their independence.

The changes in the company, the arrival of women and slaves, and the creation of the House of Burgesses all played a role in the growth of Virginia. People continued to arrive in the colony. More and more land was cleared to plant tobacco. Relations with the Indians of the area remained peaceful. The future of Virginia looked bright. However, for the London Company prosperity in the colony did not translate into enough profits to satisfy the investors. Even worse, Powhatan died in 1622 and his brother Opechancanough took over as leader of the confederacy. Opechancanough was extremely concerned with the fact that the colonists were increasing in numbers and taking whatever land they wanted.

Trouble in Virginia and England

OPECHANCANOUGH'S WAR

The growing demand for land to grow tobacco strained the peace between the Powhatan and the colonists. When Opechancanough took over the leadership of the confederacy after his brother Powhatan's death in 1618, he wanted to stop the loss of Indian lands. The tobacco boom was taking away land the Indians needed to survive. At first, Opechancanough hesitated to act. The number of colonists had grown rapidly, and he was not sure that he wanted to break his brother's peace. However, in early spring 1622, the colonists arrested and executed one of Opechancanough's warriors named Nematanou. He was accused of killing a white trader. Opechancanough had had enough.

On March 22, 1622, Opechancanough ordered a surprise attack on many of the plantations simultaneously. It was Good Friday, and the colonists were completely unprepared for the attack. By the end of the day, 347 colonists had been killed and 25 plantations around Jamestown were burned to the ground. The losses for the colony might have been even greater had not an Indian boy named Chauco warned some colonists. Chauco had become a Christian and worked on the plantation of Richard Pace.

It is said that Chauco told Pace of the attack and he got his family to safety. Then Pace got in his canoe and went two miles down the James River and warned the colonists at Jamestown. Without

C. Smith taketh the King of Pamavnkee prisoner 1608

Opechancanough, Powhatan's brother, became leader of the Powhatan after his brother's death. In this image, Captain Smith threatens Opechancanough's life unless the American Indian pays the colonists by providing corn for them. *(Library of Congress, Prints and Photographs Division [LC-USZ62-31735])*

Chauco's warning, Opechancanough might have succeeded in driving the English back into the ocean. What happened instead was almost 10 years of continuous raids on both sides. The colonists were quick to retaliate and often did not care which Indians they attacked.

A number of modern researchers have tried to estimate the population of the 26 tribes of the Powhatan Confederacy and the other Algonquian-speaking tribes of the Virginia Tidewater. The best estimates suggest that there were almost 15,000 Algonquian-speaking Indians in Virginia in 1610. Through warfare and disease, their population fell to less than 2,000 by 1670 and less than 350 by the end of the 1600s. By that time, the Indians of the Tidewater were no longer a factor. The same fate would befall the Iroquoian- and Siouan-speaking tribes in the Piedmont and the mountains of the colony.

Raids conducted by colonists were at least as vicious as the Good Friday attack by Opechancanough. The colonists would swoop down on a village, kill as many Indians as they could, then burn the village and the crops growing around it. Opechancanough and his followers continued to fight as well, making Virginia an extremely dangerous place to live.

From this point forward, the practice in Virginia was one that today would be called genocide. An organized and concerted effort was made to kill or drive away as many Indians as possible. Opechancanough led the resistance, but the growing numbers of colonists, that the colonists had firearms, and that his people had been reduced by disease meant he was fighting a war that he could not win. Despite a peace treaty in 1632, raids by both sides continued throughout the colonial period. In 1644, Opechancanough made a last desperate attempt to drive out the whites. Five hundred colonists died in the raids of 1644, but by this time there were close to 18,000 non-Indians in the colony. Opechancanough, who was reportedly more than 100 years old by this time, was captured and shot by one of the colonists guarding him.

THE END OF THE LONDON COMPANY

The most surprising victim of Opechancanough's War was the London Company. Failure to provide any profits to its investors and the sudden Indian uprising caused King James I to start proceedings against the company to revoke its charter. After a ruling in the

Charles I ruled England, Ireland, and Scotland from 1625 until his execution in 1649. *(Library of Congress, Prints and Photographs Division [LC-USZ62-91613])*

king's favor by the courts, the London Company lost its charter. At first, James I wanted to reorganize a new company to take over the colony of Virginia. However, James I died on March 27, 1625, before the commission he had set up had decided how to proceed.

James I's son Charles I became king. Charles I decided to resolve the situation in Virginia in a direct fashion. Six weeks after taking the throne, Charles I declared Virginia a royal colony. The royal colony of Virginia extended from what is now Pennsylvania all the way to Spanish Florida, and from the Atlantic to the Pacific Ocean.

As a royal colony, Virginia was directly under the authority of the king and his government. A royal governor was appointed. For the next 150 years, a succession of governors appointed in London were in charge of Virginia. Some of these governors did a good job and got along with the House of Burgesses and the people of the colony; others did not. During this time, as Virginia grew and prospered, the people in the colony became more and more self-sufficient and less dependent on England.

CARVING UP VIRGINIA

Charles I had included a huge amount of land in the royal colony of Virginia when he took it over. However, within a few years he granted additional charters that drastically reduced the size of Virginia. In 1629, Charles I, king of England, granted all the land in North America between latitudes 31° and 36° north to Sir Robert Heath, the attorney general of England at the time. Heath did little with his grant. The land was called Carolina after the king. The only settlers who actually headed for Carolina at the time landed in Virginia. They decided it would be easier to settle there than try and carve their own settlement out of the wilderness.

The other piece of the royal colony that Charles I gave away was north of the settlements in Virginia. In 1632, Lord Baltimore, a Catholic nobleman in England, was granted the land in Virginia north of the Potomac River to create a haven for Catholics who wanted to leave England. Lord Baltimore called his colony Maryland. By 1680, only the Massachusetts and Virginia colonies had more people than Lord Baltimore's colony. It was not until Charles I's son became king in 1660 and a new grant for Carolina was drawn up that settlement took place there. In between, England went through a number of upheavals.

TROUBLE IN ENGLAND

The original settlers in the Plymouth and Massachusetts colonies had been religious dissidents from England. The Church of England was the official church at the time, and many thought that it needed to be changed. They felt its practices and beliefs needed to be purified to more closely adhere to the ideas of the Protestant Reformation. It was because of this that those who disagreed with the Church of England became known as Puritans. Many Puritans argued that the Church of England was beyond salvaging and left for North America. Others stayed in England in hopes of reforming the church.

George Calvert, the first Lord Baltimore, was given some land that had been part of Virginia from Charles I in 1632. *(National Archives of Canada)*

By the 1640s, the situation in England turned into a full-blown civil war. Oliver Cromwell led the Puritans, and Charles I was the leader of the forces loyal to the Crown and the church. Cromwell turned out to be an excellent military leader, and in 1649 he was able to defeat the forces of the king. The king was captured and executed. Cromwell was selected by the Puritans to run the government as Lord Protector.

In 1641, Charles I had appointed Sir William Berkeley the royal governor of Virginia. Berkeley's leadership had a far-reaching impact on the colony. He worked with the leading planters of the

Oliver Cromwell was a Puritan and military leader who eventually became Lord Protector of England. *(Library of Congress, Prints and Photographs Division [LC-USZ62-95711])*

colony to ensure they continued to support him. In addition, he became a planter himself, so that his interests were often served by siding with Virginia. During his first term he was very popular.

After Charles I was captured and executed, many of his supporters, known as Cavaliers, chose to go to Virginia rather than live under the government of the Puritans. With its growing landed gentry and the fact that many English people had settled there, it was the colony that was most like home to them. With Berkeley still in charge, the Church of England as the official church, and the influx of Cavaliers, Virginia was seen by Cromwell and others in his government as a potential problem.

The trade that flowed in and out of Virginia was extremely important to the government in London, whether it was royalist or Puritan. In 1651, the Parliament under Cromwell passed a law intended to ensure that the government got as much benefit as

Sir William Berkeley
(1606–1677)

Sir William Berkeley, like many who had come to Virginia in the early days of the colony, was the younger son of a member of the British nobility. His father, Sir Maurice Berkeley, and his older brother John, Lord Berkeley, were staunch supporters of the Stuart monarchy. They were able to get Sir William appointed governor of Virginia. For William Berkeley, being the governor of Virginia was his chance to become successful in his own right. He became a wealthy planter as well as governor.

His loyal support of the Stuart monarchy eventually turned the people of Virginia against him during his second term as governor. He eventually fell from favor with many Virginians, but it was during his time as governor that Virginia grew into the premier English colony in North America.

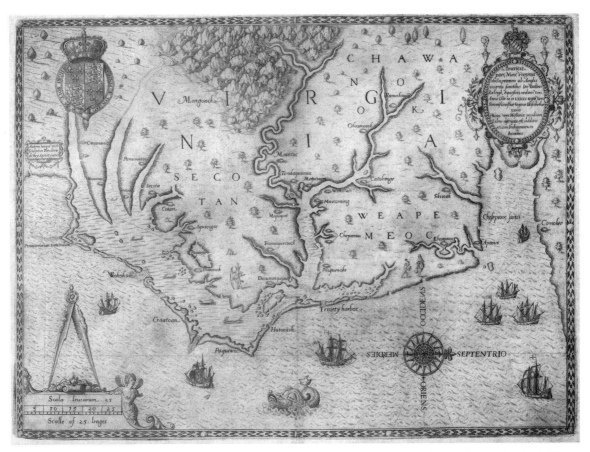

In this 1580s map of Virginia based on an engraving by Theodor de Bry, Virginia's coastline is clearly visible. *(Library of Congress, Prints and Photographs Division [LC-USZ62-54020])*

possible from trade with Virginia and other colonies. Known as the Navigation Acts of 1651, these laws required that all trade between England and its colonies be carried in English-made ships with crews made up of at least 50 percent English sailors. This was meant to ensure that goods from Virginia and elsewhere would be sent back to England and not to other countries in Europe.

In addition, the Puritans wanted to make sure that Virginia was under their control. In March 1652, a fleet of English naval ships arrived in Chesapeake Bay. The commissioners on board the ships had been sent by Cromwell with instructions to try and get the cooperation of Berkeley, the royal governor, through negotiation. If that failed, they were to use whatever means necessary.

Berkeley, like his father and brother and many of the colonists in Virginia, was loyal to the Stuart monarchy and the Church of England. Berkeley refused to step aside peacefully. However, when the ships sailed up to Jamestown and threatened to turn their cannons on the town, Berkeley had little choice but to surrender. It was one thing to defeat an outnumbered force of Indians with bows and arrows. It was a whole other situation to defy what at the time was the most powerful navy in the world.

The Puritans had too many problems at home to turn much attention on Virginia. Once Berkeley had stepped down as governor and retired to his plantation, Cromwell and Parliament were happy to leave the Virginians alone to continue growing tobacco. By 1660, there were more than 27,000 people in the colony who took advantage of the preoccupation of the Puritans to continue their development of local government and their identity as Virginia. The idea that they were Virginians first and English second would continue to grow. It would ultimately fuel the move toward independence 100 years later.

It was during this time that a number of Virginia's towns and cities were established. Alexandria, Fredericksburg, Richmond, and Petersburg all started out as tobacco trading centers for those who were moving into the Piedmont as the best land in the Tidewater was already taken. Some of the Tidewater planters were also buying land inland as tobacco quickly depleted the fertility of the original fields where it had been planted.

5

Restoration and Rebellion

THE RESTORATION OF
THE STUART MONARCHY

In 1660, the Puritans were driven out of power in England by royalist supporters of the Stuart monarchy. Charles II, Charles I's son, became king. Virginia was once again destined to be a royal colony. On hearing of the restoration of the monarchy, the House of Burgesses voted to have William Berkeley resume his role as governor, an act that was confirmed by Charles II. However, Charles II had many debts to pay and looked to North America to reward those who had been loyal to him.

The Carolina grant was transferred to eight of Charles II's loyal followers. The lands claimed by the Dutch between the Delaware and Connecticut Rivers were granted to his brother James. James in turn gave what would become New Jersey to another group of Stuart supporters. Later, William Penn used the debts owed to his father's estate to get the grant that would become the colonies of Pennsylvania and Delaware. Charles II's reign became a time of relative calm in England when the Crown could devote more attention to its colonies in North America.

NAVIGATION ACT OF 1660

To strengthen the Crown's control of trade in its colonies around the world, especially those in North America, Parliament passed

Charles II
(1630–1685)

Charles II was 19 years old when his father was executed in 1649. Charles, his brother James, and many of his father's supporters were forced to leave England. Scotland and parts of Ireland recognized Charles as king, and in 1651 he invaded England from Scotland with an army of 10,000. As Charles made his way south, people turned out to greet his army and proclaim him king. However, on September 3, 1651, Charles's army was defeated by Oliver Cromwell in a battle near the English town of Worcester.

Charles fled to France where he lived in poverty until he returned as king after a royalist army defeated the Puritans. Before he could take the throne he was forced to give more power to Parliament. Charles II ruled from 1660 until his death in 1685. During his reign, life in England was relatively calm; however, Charles was constantly in need of money to support his lavish lifestyle as king. He may have been trying to make up for the years he had lived in poverty in exile.

Charles II ruled England, Scotland, and Ireland from 1660 until his death in 1685. *(Library of Congress, Prints and Photographs Division [LC-USZ62-96910])*

another Navigation Act in 1660. This one went a step further. This law stated that not only must products like tobacco, rice, and indigo (a plant used as a dye) travel in English ships (this included ships from the English colonies), they could be traded only within the English colonies or directly with England. The law also required that the crews be 75 percent English instead of 50 percent. This was unpopular in Virginia, which was shipping some of its tobacco to other European countries where a higher price was paid.

In many ways, the closed trade system that tried to restrict trade to the benefit of England was an underlying cause in the independence movement more than 100 years later. Tobacco and other agricultural products often brought a higher price outside of the British Empire. At the same time, commodities like sugar and tea, which were imported into the American colonies, were cheaper if bought from non-English producers. During the next 100 years, many American colonial merchants, planters, and manufacturers would be involved in illegal trade in one way or another. When England tried to put a stop to the smuggling and raised taxes on trade in the colonies in the 1760s and 1770s, a revolution was created that would cost England all its colonies in North America except for Canada, which it had taken from the French.

BACON'S REBELLION

Virginia in the early 1670s was really two different places. The Tidewater was dotted with large estates owned by wealthy tobacco planters who controlled the politics of the colony. Governor

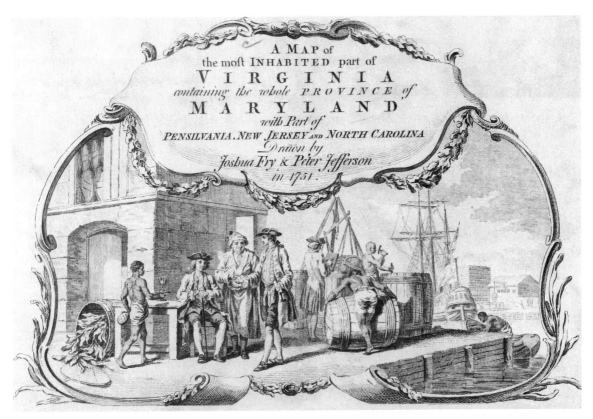

This detail of a 1752 map shows a wharf used to ship tobacco. *(Library of Congress)*

William Berkeley was the shining example of this group. He believed in a privileged class of landowners, and his plantation Green Spring was one of the finest in Virginia. In addition to being a politician and planter, the governor had used his position to control the profitable trade with the Indians of the Piedmont. The Susquehannock who had left Pennsylvania and moved into Maryland and Virginia were also involved.

Recent arrivals who could not afford to buy what little Tidewater land was left moved west of the fall line. In addition, many former indentured servants who had completed their time of service moved west. Many of these people disliked the wealthy planters and politicians who controlled the colony. Along with the problems caused by this social and geographic division of the colony, there was also the situation with the Indians.

The Indians of the Tidewater had long since been killed or forced to move to the west. For the large plantations, thievery by former indentured servants was a much bigger concern than any Indian problems. However, along the frontier there were constant skirmishes between the encroaching colonists and the retreating Indians. The conflict between frontier settlers and Indians boiled over in July 1675. What started between the frontier colonists and their Indian enemies led to a regional and class struggle between the different factions of Virginia colonists.

Thomas Mathew was a plantation owner in Stafford County near Fredericksburg who frequently traded with the nearby Doeg Indians. In July 1675, some of the Doeg were cheated when Mathew refused to pay them for goods they had sold to him. To get what was due them, the Doeg slipped onto the Mathew plantation early in the morning and stole some hogs. In the raid, they also killed Mathew's farm foreman, or overseer.

When the local militia leaders heard of the raid and the death of the overseer, they called out the militia and went after the Doeg and the stolen hogs. They pursued the Indians into nearby Maryland, where they killed some members of the Doeg tribe. They also killed some Susquehannock who had absolutely nothing to do with the raid. Other Susquehannock sought revenge for their murdered tribe members and conducted a number of raids along the Virginia-Maryland border.

Word traveled slowly back to Jamestown of the problems on the frontier. Even when Governor Berkeley was made aware of the growing conflict on the frontier, he hesitated to take quick action. Some have speculated that his slow response was based on his age and diminishing abilities. Others said that he was reluctant to jeopardize his relations with his Indian trading partners. Whatever the cause, it was August 31, 1675, before the governor called his council together to form a plan of action.

After seeking the advice of the council, the governor asked two men, John Washington and Isaac Allerton, to look into the situation along the frontier. If they found cause, Allerton and Washington were instructed to call up the local militia against the Indians. The two investigators skipped the investigation and went straight to the militia. They also contacted the governor of Maryland and asked for more troops.

Governor William Berkeley ruled Virginia from 1642 until 1652 and from 1660 until 1677. *(Courtesy of The Library of Virginia)*

In September, the combined force of Virginians and Marylanders came upon a large group of Susquehannock in an old fort on the Maryland side of the Potomac River. The Indians wanted to talk and sent out five of their leaders, but the colonials quickly killed the Susquehannock negotiators. The colonials had no cannons with them, so they were unable to destroy the fort. For seven weeks they kept the Susquehannock trapped in the fort, until one night the Indians left the fort, slipped past the English sentries, and disappeared into the forest.

For the rest of the fall and into 1676, the Susquehannock raided all along the northern frontier of Virginia. The worst raid was in January 1676, and left 36 colonists dead. At this point, the Susquehannock thought they had fulfilled their need to avenge their leaders who had been murdered at the fort and offered to negotiate with the governor. Berkeley, who had been slow to act against the Indians, was equally slow to forgive. The

The Susquehannock lived near the Susquehanna River, which flows from New York through Pennsylvania and empties in Chesapeake Bay in Maryland. This image of a Susquehannock man is a detail of a map drawn by Captain John Smith, who encountered the tribe in his travels. *(Library of Congress, Geography and Map Division)*

Susquehannock decided they would be better off out of the area, and they moved further into the interior. However, the other tribes along the frontier chose to finish what the colonists had started and began raiding with even more savagery than had already taken place. The Susquehannock had been satisfied to kill a few people on the frontier and take what they wanted. The new raiders killed any colonists they found, took what they could use, and burned everything else.

Again Berkeley's response was not what the people along the frontier wanted. The governor and the assembly decided to build a series of forts along the frontier and then establish patrols between the forts. This defensive tactic angered many who wanted direct action. This turned them against the governor. Although the Indians were still seen as the enemy, the divisions between the colonists were being strained by the problem.

When a rumor circulated that a large group of Indians was preparing to attack Charles City County, a call went out for volunteers to go after the Indians before they could attack. Many volunteers turned out and they sent a delegation to Jamestown to ask Berkeley to commission their expedition and provide them with leadership. Berkeley refused. At this point, Nathaniel Bacon stepped up and agreed to lead the volunteers against the rumored Indians who in fact did not exist.

Governor Berkeley saw Bacon's agreement to lead the volunteers as a betrayal. The governor sent word to Bacon that his actions bordered on mutiny against the king's authority. He ordered Bacon to return

Nathaniel Bacon
(1647–1676)

Nathaniel Bacon was born into the nobility of England at Friston Hall, Suffolk, England, in 1647. He lived the life appropriate to his position as a member of England's upper class. He went to college and law school. He also toured the other countries of Europe in his late teens. Against the objections of her family, he married Elizabeth Duke in 1670. She was immediately disowned by her father.

After being involved in some possibly illegal attempts to make money, Nathaniel Bacon took his wife and headed to Virginia. In 1674, they arrived in Virginia, where he had a number of relatives. Both the colony's auditor general, who was also named Nathaniel Bacon, and Governor William Berkeley were his cousins. In August 1674, the recently arrived Bacon bought a plantation that was 40 miles upriver from Jamestown in Henrico County. Six months after he arrived in Virginia, his cousin, the governor, appointed him to fill an empty seat on the governor's council. It was unprecedented that someone so new to the colony would be given such a prestigious and powerful position. Bacon's role in the rebellion that bears his name is considered by many to be a first important step on the road to independence. Over time, many

have questioned Bacon's motivation and objectives in the short time he was in Virginia. His sudden death from dysentery in October 1676, and the lack of any written records that Bacon might have left behind, have left scholars somewhat baffled.

Nathaniel Bacon moved from London, England, to Virginia in 1674. Two years later, he led a rebellion named after him that disagreed with Governor William Berkeley's policy toward Native Americans. *(Library of Congress, Prints and Photographs Division [LC-USZ62-91133])*

to Jamestown. Instead Bacon rounded up more volunteers and headed for the frontier. The governor called out his own force and went after Bacon, but arrived too late to stop him.

Built in 1655 and known as "Bacon's Castle," this building in Surrey County, Virginia, was seized during the rebellion and used as a fort. *(Library of Congress, Prints and Photographs Division [HABS, VA, 91-_,1-31])*

Berkeley returned to Jamestown in a state of extreme anger at being defied by his much younger cousin. He officially had him removed from the council and publicly had Bacon declared a rebel. While this was going on, Bacon and his volunteer army were on

the frontier near modern-day Clarksville, hunting Indians.

The force came upon a village of friendly Occaneechee, who told Bacon that there was a group of Susquehannock nearby. The Occaneechee participated in the successful attack on the Susquehannock. Although the record is not clear, after the attack it appears that Bacon's followers argued with the Occaneechee over the goods that were captured from the Susquehannock. In the end, the colonials did what they had set out to do and killed Indians, including their recent allies the Occaneechee. To many along the frontier, Bacon was seen as a hero.

The governor called for an assembly election, the first in 14 years, to deal with Bacon's Rebellion and the Indian problem. The people of Henrico County surprised the governor by electing Bacon to the House of Burgesses. Bacon was leery of returning to Jamestown to take his seat in the assembly, so he sailed down the James River from his plantation in his private sloop with 50 armed men as an escort. When he arrived, the governor had no intention of allowing Bacon to take his seat, and had the town's gunners fire at the sloop. That night, Bacon slipped into town to meet with some of his allies. He was captured the next day, as he tried to sail home, by an armed merchant ship that had been commissioned by the governor to pursue him.

To everyone's surprise, the governor pardoned Bacon on June 9, 1676. He also restored him to the council and promised to give him a commission to continue the campaign to secure the frontier. Considering the later reversals and problems between the two men, many wonder why the governor acted as he did. It may have been that he saw popular opinion swinging away from him and his few remaining allies among the colony's elite planters.

On June 23, 1676, Bacon had become impatient waiting for the governor to give him his commission. Bacon rode into Jamestown with 500 militia to support him and surrounded the capitol. The governor sent out a representative to see what Bacon wanted. Bacon replied that he wanted his commission, 30 blank commissions to give out to officers in the militia, a pardon, and his sloop back. It did not appear from his demands that he had plans to take over the government, but that is how the governor saw it. Berkeley refused to give Bacon anything while he occupied the capitol with an armed force.

Bacon's Laws

The session of the House of Burgesses that convened on June 5, 1676, lasted for 20 days and passed a series of laws that have come to be known as Bacon's Laws. They were for the most part a reaction to the problems that had brought the colony to the point where the various factions were ready to fight each other. The first of these laws threw out the governor's defensive plan of forts and patrols along the frontier. It called for an attempt to drive the remaining Indians out of Virginia or kill them.

Other laws dealt with taking Indian land and the still lucrative Indian trade. Many others were attempts to lessen the friction between the wealthy planters who had dominated the colony's politics and the small farmers of the colony. These included extending the right to vote to all freemen in the colony. One in particular seemed to be aimed at preventing another person like Nathaniel Bacon from moving in and rising to power so quickly. It required all office-holders in the colony to have lived there for at least three years. At that point, Bacon had been in the colony for little more than two years. Charles II later struck down all the laws passed by this session of the assembly. However, many of them were put back in by later assemblies.

The two men, although related only by marriage, seemed to share a similar temperament. Neither one was willing to back down. At one point, the governor rushed out on to the steps of the assembly building and offered to fight Bacon one-on-one with swords. Instead, Bacon ordered his troops to aim their rifles at the windows of the building and prepare to fire. The burgesses did what the governor would not and conceded to Bacon's demands. On June 26, General Bacon and his troops left town.

As soon as Bacon was gone, the governor declared him a traitor. Instead of continuing to the frontier to fight Indians, Bacon turned his army around and headed back to confront the governor. Berkeley tried to raise a force of his own to defend Jamestown and bring Nathaniel Bacon to justice. However, there were very few volunteers willing to fight other Virginians or to go against the popularity of Bacon.

Bacon temporarily gave up his campaign against the Indians and set up headquarters at Middle Plantation, now Williamsburg. From there, Bacon issued his "Manifesto" and "Declaration of the People" in which he condemned the governor and defended his own Indian policy. Berkeley fled across the Chesapeake. Unable to pursue him, Bacon left 800 men to hold Jamestown, and went after the last of the Pamunkey, who had been relegated to living in what the colonists called the Dragon Swamp.

After killing and capturing many of the Indians in the swamp, Bacon returned. He found that the governor had returned and pardoned the 800 men who were supposed to hold the capitol. When Bacon appeared at Jamestown, he again found his cousin in charge. Bacon saw that it would be too costly to take the town by force so he prepared for a siege. A week later, those supporting the governor escaped by ship, and Bacon's army marched into Jamestown and burned the town on September 19, 1676.

His victorious army took the opportunity to start raiding the plantations around Jamestown, while Bacon tried to figure out what to do next. Word had already reached the colony that the king was sending 1,000 soldiers and a supporting naval squadron to the colony. Bacon was in control of the colony, at least for the time being. While he was trying to decide what to do next, he became ill. On October 26, 1676, he died of dysentery. Without

Nathaniel Bacon and his followers burned Jamestown on September 19, 1676, as Governor Berkeley watched from the ship to which he had fled. *(North Wind Picture Archives)*

their fiery leader, the rebels quickly dispersed. It was time to go back to their farms and get the harvest in.

When the English forces arrived in January 1677, there was no one for them to fight. Governor Berkeley was replaced and went to England to defend himself. A number of those who fought with Bacon were arrested and executed for treason. It appeared that the Crown was once again firmly in control of its most important North American colony. However, the people of Virginia had come to see that the interests of the Crown and what was best for Virginia were not the same thing. Nathaniel Bacon had lit the match of rebellion that would take another 100 years to flame into a war for independence.

6

Growth, Expansion, and War in Virginia

Throughout the colonial period and into the early years of the United States, Virginia was the most populous of the original 13 states. By 1700, there were more than 58,000 people in Virginia, and it was growing rapidly. One hundred years later, there would be almost 900,000 people in the state. By 1700, the Tidewater area was well established and mostly controlled by large plantation owners. Contributing to the population growth during this time were black slaves imported from the Caribbean and directly from Africa, as well as slaves born on the plantations of Virginia. More than one-third, or almost 350,000, Virginians

Slaves in Virginia

The white planters of Virginia lived in some of the grandest houses in the colonies, but their African slaves lived under some of the worst conditions. They were forced to work long hours in the fields on barely enough poor food to survive. What clothing they had was of the cheapest quality available.

The houses they lived in were often little more than shacks with dirt floors. Slave owners and overseers kept the slaves working by intimidation and force when needed. Slaves were considered property and had no rights in the eyes of the courts or the government.

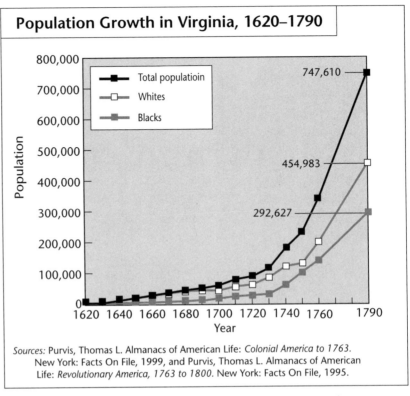

Population Growth in Virginia, 1620–1790

Sources: Purvis, Thomas L. Almanacs of American Life: *Colonial America to 1763.*
New York: Facts On File, 1999, and Purvis, Thomas L. Almanacs of American
Life: *Revolutionary America, 1763 to 1800.* New York: Facts On File, 1995.

Virginia's population grew slowly at first, but soon Virginia was the most populous colony in North America.

were slaves in 1800. At the midpoint of the 18th century, blacks made up 44 percent of the population of the colony. At the same time, in the Tidewater, slaves were more numerous than white colonists.

As the 17th century ended, Virginia was going through some changes. In 1699, after fire destroyed much of Jamestown, the capital of the colony was moved to Middle Plantation. The name of the town was changed to Williamsburg. Williamsburg was also the home of Virginia's first college: the College of William and Mary, established in 1693. It was the second college founded in the colonies. (Harvard College, founded in 1636 in Massachusetts, was the first.) Most of the new arrivals in Virginia settled in the Piedmont first and then in the Shenandoah Valley.

The College of William and Mary

In the 17th and most of the 18th century, there were very few schools in Virginia. The wealthy planters hired tutors to teach their children and prided themselves on their private libraries. The young men of these families would often go to England for college. In 1689, James Blair, a high-ranking member of the Anglican clergy in Virginia, proposed that the colony found its own college. In 1691, the assembly petitioned the Crown for a charter. In 1693, the king and queen of England, William and Mary, granted the charter. The college was named after the monarchs, and is the only college in America to have received a royal charter.

The original building for the college was designed by the famous English architect Sir Christopher Wren and it was built starting in 1695. James Blair was made the first president of the college. By 1700, Blair, two instructors, and several students lived at the college. Until 1776, the Crown continued to provide support for the college. From the time of the American Revolution until 1906, William and Mary was run as a private college. Since 1906, it has been supported in part by the state of Virginia.

The College of William and Mary's original building, shown here in a 20th-century photograph, was designed by Christopher Wren. The building burned three times before it was restored in the late 1920s. *(Library of Congress, Prints and Photographs Division [HABS, VA, 48-WIL, 4A-1])*

ECONOMIC WOES

At the end of the 17th century and during the 18th century, England was involved in four different wars with France. Virginia was not directly involved in the first three wars, which were referred to in the colonies by the name of the person sitting on the throne in England. King William's War (1689–97), Queen Anne's War (1702–13), and King George's War (1744–48) were all fought mainly in Europe and on the high seas. During the first two wars, Virginia planters suffered substantial losses of shipments of tobacco to England. At the time, the navies of both sides and numerous privately owned ships were given permission to attack enemy merchant ships wherever they found them. Even during times of peace, there were numerous pirates who attacked merchant shipping.

In 1706, for example, of the 300 ships that had tobacco as their cargo, 30 were lost to storms or were captured. Overproduction, rising costs of shipping and insurance, and loss of foreign markets all worked together to drive down profits for the tobacco growers of Virginia. Only the best-managed plantations were able to survive the recession that hit Virginia at this time.

Tobacco grown in Virginia was shipped to England in ships like the ones shown in this woodcut. *(North Wind Picture Archives)*

Pirates and Privateers

For a sailing ship in the early 18th century, the ocean was a dangerous place. Storms were impossible to predict and often sent ships to the bottom of the ocean without warning or survivors. In addition to natural disasters, the 18th century was a time of

(continues)

Born Edward Teach, Blackbeard earned his nickname as a result of his thick black beard. This image of the pirate originally appeared in an early 18th-century book titled *A General History of Pyrates*. *(North Carolina Museum of History)*

(continued)

war between the two most powerful nations in Europe—France and England. Both sides used privateers to assist their navies. A privateer was a privately owned ship that was commissioned by a government to attack the merchant ships of its enemies. The privateers' only pay was the goods and ships they captured.

At times, especially during times of peace, privateers were known to step over the line between the legal activities they were permitted and attack the ships of neutral merchants or even their own country's. At that point, privateers became pirates. The islands of the Caribbean hid many pirates who were a constant threat to shipping. Pirates operated along the coast of North America as well. In the American colonies that were still struggling to survive, pirates were often welcomed as they sold their stolen goods cheaply and paid cash for anything they needed.

Virginia was never a haven for pirates. However, shipping in the colony almost came to a stop after Queen Anne's War. Pirates led by Edward Teach, known as Blackbeard, hid in the shallow bays of North Carolina and then came out to attack ships headed to and from Virginia. In November 1718, Governor Alexander Spotswood of Virginia decided it was time to take action. Over the objection of the North Carolina governor, who many believe had a deal with the pirates, two small ships full of English naval personnel sailed into Ocracoke Bay. In the ensuing battle, Blackbeard was killed. Thirteen members of the pirate crew who survived the battle were taken back to Virginia and hanged. After Blackbeard's death, Virginia shipping had very few problems with pirates.

This further concentrated land ownership and wealth in the colony among fewer successful families. During the peace after Queen Anne's War, prices rebounded and the tobacco economy of Virginia grew to include the Piedmont as well as the plantations of the Tidewater.

Rising prices gave many smaller growers a chance to profit. Also, the Tidewater planters were constantly forced to seek additional land. Tobacco cultivation at the time quickly depleted the soil, and new ground was constantly being added. Some of the wealthiest planters owned land all over the colony. Labor shortages also contributed to the problems of Virginia at the time. Prosperity in England, better opportunities in other colonies, and Virginia's bad reputation from its early days had caused the pool of available indentured servants to dry up. More and more, Virginians turned to slavery to find workers for their plantations.

WESTWARD EXPANSION

The Piedmont was quickly filling up as Tidewater planters and small farmers grabbed land as fast as they could. Many of the people who moved into Virginia came south from Pennsylvania, which had been established as a colony by William Penn in the 1690s. But there was still not enough land to satisfy the needs and desires of Virginians. In 1716, the governor, Alexander Spotswood, learned that an easy way over the Blue Ridge Mountains had been discovered. He organized and personally led an expedition to see what was over the mountains.

The Spotswood expedition followed the Rapidan River to the base of the Blue Ridge. The governor and his party crossed the mountains through Swift Run Gap and found themselves at the Shenandoah River on September 6, 1716. They feasted on the banks of the Shenandoah and claimed the valley in the name of King George and Virginia. As settlers moved into the valley, large sections of it were taken up by planters and land speculators from the eastern part of the colony. One group received 100,000 acres near present-day Winchester, Virginia. William Beverley, one of the colony's wealthiest planters, filed on a grant of 120,000 acres near what would become Staunton. Thomas, Lord Fairfax, who had early received grants in Virginia, arrived from England in 1735 to ensure that his claim to 6 million acres was still intact.

By the middle of the 18th century, Virginia land speculators wanted more. The original grant from the colony went all the way to the Pacific. It must have seemed that some were intent on making sure Virginia stretched from sea to shining sea. A sense of urgency fueled the Virginians as word reached the English colonies that the French were intent on connecting their colony in Canada with New Orleans and their forts on the Mississippi River.

A number of land companies were formed to claim additional lands. The Ohio Company claimed 500,000 acres in what is now West Virginia. The Loyal Land Company gained control of 800,000 acres in the area of the Cumberland Gap, where modern-day Virginia, North Carolina, and Tennessee meet. Many of Virginia's most prominent citizens invested in these land companies. The Ohio Company included Governor Robert Dinwiddie,

In this wood engraving, George Washington surveys the Shenandoah Valley in 1760. The area was first claimed by Governor Alexander Spotswood and his expedition in 1716. *(Library of Congress, Prints and Photographs Division [LC-USZ62-64111])*

Richard Henry Lee, George Mason, and George Washington. It was the Ohio Company that came head to head with the French in the upper reaches of the Ohio River. The group first built a trading post and fort at Wills Creek, which is now Cumberland, Maryland. They had plans to move on to the Ohio River. However, the French had already moved into the area and it would take a war to decide who would get the lands between the Appalachian Mountains and the Mississippi River.

THE FRENCH AND INDIAN WAR

Governor Dinwiddie decided to do what was necessary to protect his interests and those of his fellow Virginians in the region of the Ohio. His first response was to send George Washington to talk to the French. Washington was 21 years old when he left Williamsburg, Virginia, on October 31, 1753, to take a message to the French at Fort Le Boeuf in what is now western Pennsylvania. Washington was a major in the Virginia militia as well as a planter and surveyor. He traveled west with a group that included Christopher Gist as his scout and two French interpreters.

Washington reached Fort Le Boeuf on December 11, 1753. After a cordial dinner with the fort's commander, Jacques Legardeur de Saint-Pierre, Washington delivered his message that the French were to leave the vicinity of the Ohio and return to New France. Saint Pierre politely refused and Washington headed back to Virginia. He reported to the governor on January 16, 1754, that he had passed the perfect site for a fort during his trip. It was on a point of land where the Allegheny and the Monongahela Rivers join to form the Ohio River.

Governor Dinwiddie took immediate action. Workers and a small militia force were sent out to build the fort. They reached the spot Washington had seen during the winter and began to clear the site. On April 16, 1754, a large French force arrived, and the Virginians building the fort were forced to surrender. The French completed the work and called their new post Fort Duquesne. Meanwhile Washington had been promoted to lieutenant colonel by the governor and was given command of a force of about 150 soldiers. They were to join the other Virginians at the fort.

Fortunately for the English colonials, not all the Indians in the area were allied with the French. Washington was warned that the French, not the Virginians, were awaiting his arrival. About 20 miles from Fort Duquesne, near present-day Uniontown, Pennsylvania, on May 28, 1754, Washington's force surprised a party from Fort Duquesne. In the battle that followed, the Virginians killed 10 of the French soldiers, including the officer in charge. This first battle of the French and Indian War is

Fort Necessity, near present-day Uniontown in southwestern Pennsylvania, was the location of the first battle of the French and Indian War. The reconstructed fort shown in this contemporary photograph, with a visitors' center visible in the background, consists primarily of a storehouse surrounded by a stockade, ditches, and mounds of dirt. *(National Park Service)*

known as the Battle of Great Meadows. It was the only victory for the English side for quite a while.

After the battle, Washington had his troops hastily build defenses that they named Fort Necessity. After a few more skirmishes between the Virginians and the French, a French force of more than 1,000 surrounded Fort Necessity on July 3, 1754. Washington had fewer than 400 troops when the battle started, and from the fort they were able to kill or wound many of the French. However, the Virginians suffered many casualties as well. More than 100 of Washington's men were either dead or wounded. The Americans inside the fort were also low on supplies. Washington realized there was nothing to be gained by trying to hold the fort, so he surrendered. Fortunately for Washington and his men, the French allowed them to return to Virginia. The French were clearly in control of the Ohio.

In January 1755, General Edward Braddock arrived in Virginia with 1,000 regular army troops, most of whom were Irish. His orders were to remove the French from the Ohio River area. Braddock enlisted George Washington as his aide and began to move his force along with all their supplies and artillery toward Fort Duquesne. Braddock had never been in the colonies and had no idea how difficult it would be to just get his army into the west.

The British expected the colonials to assist the general, and Virginia provided men and supplies. Braddock had nothing but contempt for the ill-clad and loosely disciplined colonial militia. He turned down the offer of help from Native Americans who were loyal to the British side. The government of Pennsylvania, which was controlled by Quakers, refused to take any warlike action. Benjamin Franklin, one of the political leaders in Pennsylvania, convinced the assembly to provide food and other supplies to Braddock. Franklin bought 150 Conestoga wagons and 600 horses to move the supplies to Cumberland, Maryland, where Braddock prepared his forces for their march into the wilderness.

When Braddock arrived in Virginia, he had no idea where Fort Duquesne was, nor did he realize that there was no road to take him there. On June 7, 1755, Braddock's force left Cumberland, Maryland. It was almost 100 miles from Cumberland to Fort Duquesne. The army could travel only about three miles a day as woodsmen had to cut a road through the forest. Indian scouts from Fort Duquesne must have found it easy to keep track of Braddock's progress. The scouts also made a habit of using their tomahawks on anyone who wandered into the woods away from the main force.

By the time Braddock got close to Fort Duquesne on July 9, 1755, the French had long been aware he was coming and knew exactly what his force consisted of. The French commander, Captain Daniel de Beaujeu, was extremely concerned. He had a force of approximately 700 French and Indian fighters to defend the fort, while Braddock had 1,400 men, counting the militia. In addition, Braddock had enough artillery with him to turn the wooden fort into matchsticks if the cannons were allowed to be put into place. Beaujeu saw only one chance, and that was to attack the English before they were set up.

On June 9, Captain Beaujeu came out to meet the British, who were strung out over a couple of miles of their new road. In the initial charge by the French, the British were thrown into confusion. Captain Beaujeu died in the first charge, but his subordinates rallied the French forces, who took to the woods on either side of Braddock's road. General Braddock refused to allow his men to take cover and forced them to remain in their tight formations as the French and Indians mowed them down. The battle was so intense that Braddock had four horses shot out from under him. As he sat on his fifth horse, a bullet hit the general a fatal blow.

This is known as the Battle of the Wilderness, and the English learned a costly lesson. More than 1,000 of the English and colonial soldiers were killed or wounded. The French casualties numbered fewer than 100. In the woods of North America, standing one's ground out in the open was the way to sure defeat, even with twice the men. Some have written that the remnants of Braddock's army did not stop running until they reached Philadelphia. Washington wrote, "We have been most scandalously beaten by a trifling body of men."

After the Battle of the Wilderness, it looked like the French were going to win the war. They had other victories in New York and New England, and the frontier of Virginia became easy pickings for France's Native American allies. Settlements and homesteads were raided and burned. Settlers were killed and scalped or taken prisoner.

PITT WINS THE WAR

In part because of the failure to secure the colonies, a new government came into power in London. The new prime minister was William Pitt, and he was determined to drive the French out of North America, no matter the cost. In 1758, British general John Forbes arrived in Philadelphia with 8,000 soldiers and orders to capture Fort Duquesne. Many Virginians were upset that Forbes did not land his force in their colony. George Washington was once again recruited to make his fourth trip into the west. He no doubt hoped that it would turn out better than his first three.

Although Forbes lost 300 men in his advance unit when they went against orders and got within range of the fort, the overwhelming size of his force was more than the French were willing to fight. The French blew up Fort Duquesne and headed back to the Saint Lawrence. Forbes instructed his troops to build a new fort on the site. He named it Fort Pitt after the prime minister who had

William Pitt began his service in Parliament in 1735 and gained more power until he became prime minister during the French and Indian War. *(Library of Congress, Prints and Photographs Division [LC-USZ62-55013])*

decided to win the war. The town that quickly grew up around the fort was called Pittsburgh, Pennsylvania.

After abandoning the Ohio watershed, the French also suffered defeats in New York and New England. In 1759, the British took the fight into the heart of New France, first capturing Quebec and then Montreal. Under the Treaty of Paris, which was finally signed by both sides in 1763, all of North America east of the Mississippi

River and much of what is now western Canada were united as part of the British Empire. Although the French had surrendered, many of their Indian allies were not ready to give up. An uprising led by an Indian named Pontiac that started near Detroit and spread east to the frontiers of Virginia and Pennsylvania required British troops to defeat them. The Crown decided to keep 7,500 troops in North America in case there were further uprisings. To prevent further conflict with the Indians west of the Appalachian Mountains, the Crown forbid colonists from moving west of the mountains.

7

The Road to Revolution

Virginia, more than any other colony, had committed troops and resources to winning the French and Indian War. The Virginia government had issued paper money to pay its militia and for the supplies they needed as they participated in campaigns in Pennsylvania. The paper money had put the colony in debt, and it took a number of years to pay it off. At the same time, the government in London had accumulated a huge amount of debt. Leaders on both sides of the Atlantic had little interest in solving the other's debt problems. However, many in England thought the colonies benefited the most from the defeat of the French in North America. They made it clear that the colonists should pay at least for the maintenance of the 7,500-man force that remained in the colonies.

At the same time, George III, who had become king in 1760, was interested in gaining more royal control at home and around the British Empire. The two previous kings in England, George I and George II, had been more interested in their responsibilities in Hanover (now a part of Germany)

George III ruled Great Britain and Ireland from 1760 until 1820. *(Library of Congress)*

than in what was going on in England or its colonies. George I had become king of Great Britain to succeed the last of the Stuart monarchs, Queen Anne. During the reign of the first two Hanoverian kings, much royal authority had been passed to Parliament and the various ministries. George III was determined to reverse that trend.

George III and his ministers wanted to raise money and assert royal control. By the end of the French and Indian War in 1762, many in the colonies had been born there. Many others had come from Ireland, Scotland, and the other countries of Europe. Many of these people did not consider themselves English. They thought of themselves as Virginians, Marylanders, Pennsylvanians, or residents

George III
(1738–1820)

When Queen Anne died in 1714, she had no heirs to succeed her. As the leaders of Great Britain looked around for a new person to take the throne, they were reluctant to turn to any of the remaining Stuarts because of their Catholic faith. Instead, they selected a cousin of Queen Anne's who was the elector of Hanover (now part of Germany) to become George I, king of Great Britain. George I never learned to speak English and spent much of his time in Hanover. When he did travel to England, he brought his two mistresses with him, which angered many in England. His son George II was also more interested in the affairs of Hanover, and the rule of Great Britain fell to the civil government.

George II's grandson, George, was born on June 4, 1738, in London. The first of his family to be raised and educated in England, he was very much interested in the affairs of England, even though he maintained his hereditary title as the elector of Hanover. In 1760, he succeeded his grandfather and became George III, king of Great Britain, a position he would hold until his death in 1820. George III apparently suffered from porphyria, which is a rare genetic disease that can affect the nervous system and lead to bouts of mental illness. George III had spells of apparent dementia as early as 1763. In 1788, he was so ill that Parliament passed a regency bill that allowed someone to take over when the king was unable to function. From 1811 on, his son acted as regent, as George III was considered unable to rule. It was George III and his prime minister, Lord North, who plotted the course for Great Britain that would cause the American Revolution and the loss of the 13 American colonies.

of one of the other 10 colonies first. Despite these feelings, it would take the actions of the Crown and Parliament to drive a wedge between the colonies and England that resulted in war.

THE SUGAR ACT OF 1764

George Grenville became prime minister of Great Britain in 1763. He proceeded to plan the strategy of having the colonies pay for the costs associated with administering them. He took many steps to reform the role of the customs officers to make it easier for them to collect all the duties that were owed to the Crown. Then in 1764, he had a law passed by Parliament that has become known as the Sugar Act.

The Sugar Act was enacted to put a stop to the trade in illegal molasses and sugar from outside the British Empire. For most of the people in Virginia, the Sugar Act and the other reforms to the customs collection system mattered little. The tobacco trade, which still supported most of the Virginia economy, was almost entirely conducted within the existing trade laws. However, Grenville had included language in the Sugar Act that did catch the attention of Virginia's leaders. It said, ". . . it may be proper to charge certain Stamp Duties in the said Colonies and Plantations."

In addition, Grenville got another bill through the Parliament that was aimed at Virginia. It was called the Currency Act of 1764, and it kept colonies from issuing paper money in the future. Virginia had issued paper money during the French and Indian War to fund its military efforts, and the paper money provided needed cash in the colony. The end of paper money and the threat of a stamp tax brought the House of Burgesses into action.

THE STAMP ACT OF 1765

When the House of Burgesses went into session in 1765, they worked on a plan to get around the Currency Act with no discussion of the Sugar Act or the possibility of a stamp tax. When the plan of the House of Burgesses failed to receive the support of the governor and council, the burgesses turned their attention to the stamp tax. They composed a number of letters to be sent to England. The strongest was sent to the colony's agent, Edward Montague. It instructed him to use whatever influence he had to stop the stamp tax.

Colonists denounce the Stamp Act in 1765. *(Library of Congress)*

When the Stamp Act came up for debate in the House of Commons in London, no one was allowed to read the protests from Virginia and other colonies. It was signed by George III on March 22, 1765, having passed in Parliament with almost no opposition. The Stamp Act set off such a serious reaction in the colonies that only

The Sons of Liberty

When the Stamp Act was passed by Parliament in 1765, people in the colonies formed groups in their communities to protest the act. One of the opponents of the Stamp Act in the House of Commons, Isaac Barré, called the protesters the "sons of liberty." Soon the name spread to the colonies, where it was readily adopted. Various Sons of Liberty groups organized protests against the Stamp Act and later held "tea parties" in places such as Boston, New Jersey, and South Carolina when the Tea Act of 1773 was passed.

Patrick Henry
(1736–1799)

Patrick Henry was born in Hanover County, Virginia, in 1736. His father was a surveyor and a justice on the county court. Patrick Henry was tutored by his father and received no formal education. In 1760, after unsuccessfully trying his luck in business and farming, he became a lawyer. In the courtroom, before a jury, he found his place in the world. His success in some important cases gave him enough popularity to earn him a seat in the House of Burgesses.

His exceptional skill as an orator and his radical ideas about the relationship between Great Britain and its colonies earned him a position as a Patriot leader. He is credited with being one of the architects of the Virginia Resolves. He was also elected to represent Virginia at both the First and Second Continental Congresses. He served as governor of Virginia from 1776 to 1779 and 1784 to 1786. It was at the second state convention in Richmond in 1775 that he made his most famous statement in defense of the ideas of independence from Great Britain and the need to be ready for war if necessary. At the end of the speech, he is reported to have said, "I know not what course others may take, but as for me, give me liberty or give me death."

A skilled orator, Patrick Henry represented Virginia at both continental congresses.
(Library of Congress, Prints and Photographs Division [LC-USZ62-102566])

Georgia of the thirteen colonies ever issued any stamps. In Virginia and other colonies, groups known as the Sons of Liberty were formed to lead the protests.

At the end of the House of Burgesses's session in 1765, a number of the older and more established members left for home. With barely enough members to form a quorum (the minimum needed to proceed), a group of younger members led by first-term burgess

When affixed to goods, this stamp signified that a tax must be paid upon purchase. Many colonists felt that the British unfairly introduced these taxes when they implemented the Stamp Act in 1765, which affected goods ranging from business transactions to playing cards. *(Library of Congress, Prints and Photographs Division [LC-USZ61-539])*

Patrick Henry brought up seven resolutions dealing with the Stamp Act. On May 30, 1765, five of the resolutions passed, although one of the five was rescinded the next day because, after thinking about it, a number of the burgesses felt it went too far. Collectively, the resolutions are known as the Virginia Resolves.

Although only four of the seven passed, all of the original resolutions found their way onto the pages of newspapers throughout the colonies. In Virginia, the only paper had been shut down by the governor, but in other colonies the Virginia Resolves became the model for protests of the Stamp Act. Many other colonies passed similar resolutions, and protests were held in the streets throughout the colonies. One idea of the Virginia Resolves, that it was illegal for Parliament to tax people without their consent, became a simple slogan: "No taxation without representation!"

In Virginia and throughout the colonies, those who had volunteered to be stamp agents saw effigies, or models, of themselves carried through the streets by angry mobs who would then hang and burn the effigies. George Mercer of Virginia and many other stamp agents resigned their positions rather than face the mobs. The stamps intended for Virginia were put on a British naval ship that was stationed along the North American coast and were never brought ashore. The stamps were supposed to go on printed materials, legal documents, and some consumer goods, such as playing cards. Without stamps, ships were unable to clear a harbor and legal cases were put on hold. In other colonies, some newspapers continued to publish without stamps.

A number of states sent delegates to a Stamp Act Congress in New York in October 1765. The governor in Virginia prevented the colony from sending representatives by refusing to allow the House of Burgesses to convene to select delegates. In Virginia, the newspaper stayed closed, but some of the courts declared the Stamp Act illegal and went back into session.

The protest in the colonies worked. In 1766, Parliament repealed the Stamp Act. However, in doing so they passed the Declaratory Act, which said they had the right to pass whatever laws they thought necessary to regulate the colonies.

THE TOWNSHEND DUTIES OF 1767

One of the major arguments that colonial leaders such as Ben Franklin made against the Stamp Act was that it was a direct tax on people who were not represented in Parliament. With the failure of the Stamp Act, Parliament next decided to try a series of duties on goods imported into the colonies. They believed that this type of indirect tax would be more acceptable to people. These duties were proposed by Charles Townshend who was in charge of finances for the Crown.

The Townshend Duties passed on June 29, 1767, and put duties on paper, tea, lead, glass, and painter's colors that were imported into the colonies. At first, the colonists were unsure of how to react. At the urging of a number of radical Patriot leaders, a movement grew to boycott English goods, especially those taxed under the Townshend Duties. As the boycott spread throughout the colonies, the leaders in Virginia agreed to join it. However, it had very little real impact on business in Virginia. The tobacco growers in both Virginia and Maryland were too deeply involved in the cycle of credit and tobacco to change the way they did business.

At the same time, in the large cities of New York and Boston where British troops were stationed, the protests turned violent. In New York, off-duty soldiers were taking work away from many colonials. On January 18, 1770, a large crowd of unemployed workers clashed with British soldiers at what is known as the Battle of Golden Hill. A number of people on both sides were injured in the fighting. Then on March 5, 1770, a crowd of approximately 400 protestors in Boston were taunting the soldiers guarding the customs house and throwing ice and snowballs at them. The soldiers threatened to shoot the protestors. Then someone yelled "Fire!" and the soldiers shot into the crowd. Five people were killed by the soldiers' musket fire. This was called the Boston Massacre.

Paul Revere's engraving of the Boston Massacre depicts the event that many consider the beginning of the struggle for independence. It occurred on March 5, 1770. *(Library of Congress, Prints and Photographs Division [LC-USZ62-35522])*

In the next month, April 1770, with Lord North now prime minister all the Townshend Duties except the one on tea were repealed. It appeared to be another victory for the Patriot movement. Following the repeal of the Townshend Duties, the colonies remained relatively quiet until Lord North and others in the government decided to help the struggling East India Company.

THE TEA ACT OF 1773

The British East India Company had exclusive rights to bring tea from Asia and India to England. From there, tea was exported throughout the rest of the British Empire, which included the American colonies. The fact that the tea had to go to middlemen in England before it went to the American colonies made it very expensive. It was much cheaper to drink tea that was smuggled into the colonies from Dutch colonies. Many officials in the government in London and in Parliament had an interest in the East India Company, and to keep it out of bankruptcy, they passed the Tea Act on May 10, 1773.

The Tea Act allowed the East India Company to ship tea directly to the American colonies, avoiding the wholesalers in England. This would have actually made English tea cheaper, and it was thought no American would object. However, the law gave the East India Company a monopoly on the tea business in the colonies. It became just the cause that people like the Sons of Liberty were looking for. On December 16, 1773, when the first shipment of tea arrived in Boston, 60 members of the Sons of Liberty disguised as Indians boarded three ships and dumped 340 cases of tea into the harbor. The incident became known as the Boston Tea Party. Similar events occurred in Maryland, New Jersey, and South Carolina, and a general tea boycott spread throughout the colonies.

THE INTOLERABLE ACTS OF 1774

Parliament and the Crown had had enough. George III and Lord North decided it was time to teach the upstart colonials of Boston a lesson. Parliament proceeded to enact five new laws that were called

To protest the passage of the Tea Act, some male colonists, disguised as American Indians, boarded three ships in Boston Harbor on December 16, 1773, and dumped hundreds of cases of tea into the harbor. The event became known as the Boston Tea Party. *(Library of Congress)*

John Murray, Lord Dunmore, served as royal governor of New York in 1770 and became governor of Virginia the following year. *(Library of Congress, Prints and Photographs Division [LC-USZ62-79])*

the Coercive Acts in England. In the colonies, they were called the Intolerable Acts. The first of these acts, known as the Boston Port Bill (March 31, 1774), closed Boston Harbor until the city paid £10,000 for the destroyed tea. The second law was called the Massachusetts Government Act (May 20, 1774), and it made major changes to the charter of the colony to force more Crown control on the people of Massachusetts. The other three acts dealt with taking authority away from local courts in the colonies, the quartering of British troops in the colonies, and giving special privileges to Canada, which had not participated in any of the protests.

People throughout the colonies were outraged and frightened by this show of force by the Crown. They reasoned that if it could happen in Boston, it could happen to them as well. Many colonies sent food and other needed goods to Boston by various routes to avoid the blockade of the harbor.

In Virginia, the members of the House of Burgesses were extremely sympathetic to the plight of the people of Boston. The port of Boston was scheduled to be closed on June 1, 1774. On May 24, 1774, the House of Burgesses voted unanimously to make June 1 a day of fasting and prayer in support of the people of Boston. John Murray, Lord Dunmore, the governor, dissolved the House of Burgesses for its show of support for the Boston rebels. The burgesses moved down the street to the Raleigh Tavern and discussed their next move. It was decided that they would hold a state convention on August 1, 1774, to discuss further actions.

THE FIRST CONTINENTAL CONGRESS (1774)

On August 1, 1774, delegates from around Virginia returned to the Raleigh Tavern in Williamsburg for what would be called the First Virginia Convention. Most of the delegates were the same representatives who had served in the now dissolved House of Burgesses. They discussed the ideas of not importing or exporting any goods to or from England after November 1, 1774. This would be a hard choice for many tobacco growers, but in the end they agreed that the principles of liberty were more important. They also agreed that Virginia should send delegates to a congress of all thirteen colonies to be held in Philadelphia beginning on September 5, 1774.

Virginia sent seven delegates to Philadelphia for what is called the First Continental Congress. They were Richard Bland, Benjamin Harrison, Patrick Henry, Richard Henry Lee, Edmund Pendleton, Peyton Randolph, and George Washington. When they arrived in Philadelphia, Randolph was elected president of the congress and Patrick Henry set the tone for the meeting by declaring, "The distinctions between Virginians, Pennsylvanians, New Yorkers, and New Englanders are no more. I am not a Virginian, but an American!"

Despite radicals like Henry urging that the colonies should prepare for war, most of the delegates hoped to reconcile the problems between the colonies and the Crown. The congress debated and finally passed 10 resolutions outlining what the delegates thought were the rights of colonial governments. They also laid out a policy of embargoes against importing English goods and an embargo against exporting goods to England. They also agreed to come back to Philadelphia in spring 1775 to reevaluate the crisis between the colonies and the Crown.

Before the Second Continental Congress could meet, the situation changed drastically as fighting broke out in Massachusetts between local militia and British troops from Boston. The Battles of Lexington and Concord on April 19, 1775, made the idea of a peaceful reconciliation between the two sides unlikely.

Richard Henry Lee was one of seven delegates to represent Virginia at the First Continental Congress. *(Library of Congress, Prints and Photographs Division [LC-USZ62-92331])*

8

The War for Independence

In March 1775, the Second Virginia Convention met at John's Church in Richmond. It was at this meeting on March 23 that Patrick Henry declared, "Give me Liberty, or give me death!" After his speech, the convention agreed to start organizing a colonial militia just in case there was war with Britain. Patrick Henry was named to command the militia, and one of his first goals was to secure a large quantity of gunpowder that was stored in Williamsburg. Governor Dunmore did not want the

Loyalists and Patriots

At the beginning of the American Revolution, it is estimated that about one-third of the people in the colonies remained loyal to the Crown. They were known as Loyalists. Another third were willing to defy the Crown no matter what it took. They were called Patriots. The final third were still neutral. However, in some colonies, such as Virginia and Massachusetts, a majority believed in the Patriot cause and there were fewer Loyalists than in some colonies. The clashes between Patriots and Loyalists in Virginia were often violent, and many Loyalists lost their plantations and other businesses. Still other Loyalists lost their lives for going against the Patriot majority.

During the Second Virginia Convention, Patrick Henry delivered the speech in which he proclaimed, "Give me Liberty, or give me death!," an event depicted in this Currier & Ives lithograph. *(Library of Congress, Prints and Photographs Division [LC-USZC2-2452])*

powder to get into the hands of the militia, so on April 20, 1775, he had it moved to the *Magdalen*, a British naval ship.

On hearing of this, many militia units began to march toward Williamsburg. Many in the capital were not ready for armed conflict in the streets of their town. They were able to stop Henry and the militia when they were only a few miles away from town. Governor Dunmore was so concerned about his own personal safety that he moved onto the *Fowey*, another naval ship that was anchored off the coast of Virginia. From there, he moved to Norfolk, which was the center of Loyalist activity in Virginia.

The Second Continental Congress convened on May 10, 1775, and remained in session until the newly independent nation had a constitution. *(National Archives, Still Picture Records, NWDNS-148-CCD-35)*

THE SECOND CONTINENTAL CONGRESS (1775–1789)

When the Second Continental Congress convened on May 10, 1775, the talk of embargoes and nonimportation was pushed aside. The fighting in Boston was likely to spread, and the Continental Congress decided that it was its responsibility to organize the colonies for war. In mid-June, the congress voted to form a continental army. When the delegates looked around for a person to be put in charge of the new army, they believed there was one man who had distinguished himself in the French and Indian War who seemed like the best choice. George Washington was appointed commanding general of the new Continental army. He served in that position until the end of the war in 1781.

The Second Continental Congress became the government for the thirteen colonies and took charge of the war against England. The colonists had given the delegates the authority to do this, but in the eyes of the Crown, they were rebels committing treason. Before General Washington even got started, a major battle was fought in Boston. Colonial militia from Massachusetts and the surrounding colonies took up a position on Bunker Hill in Charlestown, Massachusetts, overlooking Boston Harbor. On June 17, 1775, when the British saw more than 1,000 colonials dug in on the top of the hill, their commander, General William Howe, sent 2,000 of his best troops to drive them out.

The British lined up at the base of the hill in their sparkling red uniforms and marched up the hill in formation. The Americans mowed them down with musket fire and the British were forced to retreat. The British regrouped and charged again and again. On the third assault, the Americans were forced to retreat as they were running out of gunpowder. The British took the hill, but they suffered huge casualties—226 dead and 828 wounded. The Americans lost 140 dead and 271 wounded. They may have lost the hill, but in many ways the Battle of Bunker Hill was seen as a victory for the Americans. They had stood their ground as they were attacked by professional, well-trained, and well-equipped British soldiers.

General Washington was soon dispatched to Boston to lead the fight against the British who were in the city. In March 1776, Washington gained the advantage over the British when he was able to place cannons from Fort Ticonderoga in New York on Dorchester Heights, a strategic area in Boston. On March 17,

The Battle of Bunker Hill on June 17, 1775, helped the colonists realize that they might have a chance at becoming independent from the British.
(Library of Congress)

1776, the British forces abandoned Boston by ship and went to Halifax, Nova Scotia, to await reinforcements. Washington headed to New York as he correctly assumed that would be the next target of the British. As Washington pursued the war in the North, fight-

George Washington commanded the Continental army during the Revolutionary War. In this image, Washington receives a salute on the field during the Battle of Trenton. *(National Archives/DOD, War & Conflict, #69)*

ing had broken out in Virginia and the Continental Congress prepared to declare independence.

GOVERNOR DUNMORE AND THE LOYALISTS

When Governor Dunmore abandoned Williamsburg, the state convention elected a Committee of Safety to head the Patriot government in Virginia. From his base in Norfolk, Dunmore used the British naval ships and personnel as well as a small force of British soldiers under his command to raid Patriot plantations along the Tidewater. The governor angered many Virginians who might not have yet chosen sides when he issued a proclamation offering freedom to any and all slaves who would run away and join his force. Slave uprisings had happened in other colonies and were always a concern for Virginians. Provoking the slaves of Virginia lost the governor more than he gained as many fearful planters joined the

Governor Dunmore fled from Williamsburg to the *Fowey,* a ship anchored off the Virginia coast, leaving the Loyalists in Williamsburg to defend themselves against Patrick Henry and the Patriot militia he led in search of gunpowder to fight the British. *(Library of Congress, Prints and Photographs Division [LC-USZC2-6371])*

Patriot cause. The Committee of Correspondence decided to act against the governor. They sent a force under the command of William Woodford to try and contain Dunmore's activities.

Woodford moved toward Norfolk and then stopped on the high ground overlooking Great Bridge on the Elizabeth River about 12 miles from Norfolk. On December 8, 1775, Governor Dunmore moved out of Norfolk with a force made up of runaway slaves, Loyalist militia, seamen and marines from the navy ships, and 200 British regular-army troops. If he had used his naval support and better managed his ground forces, Dunmore would probably have won the battle of Great Bridge. As it was, he was routed by the Americans on December 9 and was forced to retreat.

As the Americans swarmed into Norfolk, the governor and most of his Loyalist supporters crowded onto the navy ships and sailed away. The Patriots burned much of the town as Woodford and the other officers were not able to control the militia troops. From the sea, Dunmore continued to raid plantations until disease and overcrowding on the ships forced them to sail away to New York in July 1776. Loyalist activity in the colony was never again as well organized after many of the Loyalists left.

DECLARING INDEPENDENCE

On May 15, 1776, the Virginia Convention voted to "declare the United Colonies free and independent states, absolved from all allegiance to, or dependence upon, the Crown or Parliament of Great Britain." The convention also directed its delegates to the Continental Congress to work toward a declaration of independence.

After declaring independence, the State Convention turned its attention to creating a constitution for Virginia. A group was formed to draft the document, and among them was George Mason, a planter neighbor of George Washington's in Fairfax County. Mason is given credit for being the primary writer of the first document to come out of the committee that was working on a constitution. Known as the Virginia Declaration of Rights, it would have a profound influence on the Declaration of Independence and the Bill of Rights.

When the delegates from Virginia returned to the Continental Congress after Virginia had declared independence, they worked for a declaration of independence for the congress. Richard Henry Lee

George Mason
(1725–1792)

George Mason was born in Fairfax County, Virginia, in 1725. His parents were successful planters, and Mason grew up with all the privileges that were part of life for Virginia's landed aristocracy. Educated by private tutors, he, like Thomas Jefferson and many other planters of the time, was well schooled in the classics. His plantation, Gunston Hall, on the shores of the Potomac River, was considered one of the grandest of the colonial plantation houses, and still stands today. As a delegate to the Virginia State Convention, Mason was called upon to help write a constitution for the state shortly after it had declared independence. Mason is given credit for writing the Virginia Declaration of Rights, which would have an impact on the Declaration of Independence and the Bill of Rights. As a delegate from Virginia to the Constitutional Convention in 1787, he fought against the strong federal system that ended up in the Constitution, which he refused to sign. He felt somewhat vindicated when his Virginia Declaration of Rights was used as a model for the Bill of Rights that was added to the Constitution as the first 10 amendments in 1791. He died at Gunston Hall in 1792.

Gunston Hall, George Mason's best-known plantation, is a spectacular example of a colonial plantation home. Built in the 1750s and located in Fairfax County, Virginia, it is shown here in a 1981 photograph. *(Library of Congress, Prints and Photographs Division [HABS, Va,30-LORT,1-13])*

Thomas Jefferson represented Virginia at the Second Continental Congress and later served as the third president of the United States. *(National Archives/ DOD, War & Conflict, #66)*

made the initial motion for independence, and it fell to his fellow Virginia delegate Thomas Jefferson to write it. Passage of the declaration was not automatic. It was considered so important that the delegates decided that all 13 delegations needed to vote in favor of it.

When a preliminary count was taken of the delegations on the Declaration of Independence, there were nine states in favor, two opposed, and the New York delegates could not say how they would vote until they got further instructions from home. The two opposing votes came from Pennsylvania and South Carolina. The South Carolina delegates, after finding out how the other delegations would vote, said that they would not stand alone and they would vote in favor when the actual vote came. One of the Pennsylvania delegates, a Quaker, was opposed to the Declaration of Independence on the grounds of his pacifism. Instead of blocking the declaration, he left the convention, and

One of the first and boldest acts of the Second Continental Congress was to compose and sign the Declaration of Independence in summer 1776. *(Library of Congress)*

Pennsylvania was now ready to vote in favor. The New York delegates still had not received official word from home but assured the congress that they, too, would vote in favor of the Declaration of Independence.

Thomas Jefferson
(1743–1826)

Next to Washington, Jefferson may be the most famous of the American Patriots. He was born in 1743, on what was at the time the frontier of Virginia in Albemarle County. His mother, Jane Randolph Jefferson, was a member of one of the colony's wealthiest families. In 1745, her cousin William Randolph died, and his will requested that Thomas Jefferson's father, Peter, move his family to the Randolph plantation of Tuckahoe to manage the estate and raise the four Randolph children. It was under the instruction of the tutors at Tuckahoe that Jefferson began his education. Later he would attend some of the best schools in Virginia, including the College of William and Mary. After graduating when he was 19, he studied law.

Throughout his life, Jefferson continued his interests in learning. He was interested in architecture, among many other subjects, and his plantation, Monticello, and the buildings he designed at the University of Virginia still stand as an example of the diversity of his knowledge. In addition to writing the Declaration of Independence, Jefferson served Virginia and the United States throughout his life as a burgess, governor, ambassador, secretary of state under Washington, vice president, and as the third president of the United States.

His most famous words were in the preamble to the Declaration of Independence which states,

We hold these truths to be self-evident, that all men are created equal, that they are endowed by their Creator with certain unalienable Rights, that among these are Life, Liberty, and the pursuit of Happiness. That to secure these rights, Governments are instituted among Men, deriving their just powers from the consent of the governed. That whenever any Form of Government becomes destructive of these ends, it is the Right of the People to alter or to abolish it, and to institute new Government, having its foundation on such principles and organizing its powers in such form, as to them shall seem most likely to effect their Safety and Happiness. Prudence, indeed, will dictate that Governments long established should not be changed for light and transient causes; and accordingly all experience hath shown that mankind are more disposed to suffer, while evils are sufferable, than to right themselves by abolishing the forms to which they are accustomed. But when a long train of abuses and usurpations pursuing invariably the same Object evinces a design to reduce them under absolute Despotism, it is their right, it is their duty, to throw off such Government, and to provide new Guards for their future security.

Thomas Jefferson is usually given credit for authorship of the Declaration of Independence, a facsimile of which is shown here. *(National Archives)*

On July 2, 1776, the congress voted 12 to 0 in favor of declaring independence. For the next two days, they debated the final language, then on July 4, 1776, the final draft of the Declaration of Independence was approved. When the declaration was later signed, the Virginia signers were George Wythe; Richard Henry Lee; Thomas Jefferson; Benjamin Harrison; Thomas Nelson, Jr.; Francis Lightfoot Lee; and Carter Braxton.

WAR IN THE NORTH

George Washington was followed north by many Virginia Patriots who would die for the cause of liberty. After success in Boston, Washington and his poorly trained and equipped Continental army suffered a number of serious defeats. They lost battle after battle in and around New York City in summer and fall 1776. They were then chased all the way across northern New Jersey before they were able to escape across the Delaware River into Pennsylvania. On December 7, 1776, Washington made it next to impossible for the British forces to follow him across the river as he made sure there were no boats left on the New Jersey side of the Delaware.

For the next year, he played a game of cat and mouse with the British as they tried to trap him in New Jersey. In fall 1777, the British changed their tactics and moved a large force to attack Philadelphia from the south. Washington was unable to stop the British at the Battle of the Brandywine on September 11, 1777, and the congress was forced to flee as the British general Lord Cornwallis marched into the city.

Washington and what was left of his army were forced to spend a miserable winter at Valley Forge, Pennsylvania. Many soldiers deserted during the very cold and snowy winter and many more went home when their commissions ended. However, events over the winter, especially the arrival of Baron

When the Revolutionary War began in 1775, Charles, Lord Cornwallis, volunteered to serve. This image of him shows him much later in life. *(National Archives, Still Picture Records, NWDNS-148-GW-463)*

Frederick von Steuben, a Prussian who volunteered to help Washington train his troops, changed the face of the Continental army. By the time they left Valley Forge in June 1778, they were much better trained and equipped. At this time, the French had been convinced to support the Americans against their old enemies the British.

The alliance with France coupled with British defeats at Saratoga, New York (October 17, 1777), and Monmouth, New Jersey (June 28, 1778), convinced the British they needed a new strategy if they were going to hold onto their American colonies. General Lord Cornwallis decided that he should take the war to the South where he believed there were large numbers of Loyalists waiting to support him.

WAR IN THE SOUTH

In summer 1778, the British gave up Philadelphia and retreated to New York City. They then turned their attention to the South. Savannah, Georgia, fell to the British on December 29, 1778. During 1779, much of the rest of Georgia was captured. Loyalists throughout the South were encouraged to attack their Patriot neighbors. Charleston, South Carolina, was captured by the British on May 12, 1780 and the British army began its march across North and South Carolina toward Virginia. General Lord Cornwallis rightly believed Virginia to be one of the hotbeds of Patriot feeling and support. He thought that if he could conquer Virginia he could end the war.

After fighting their way north, the British began their attack on Virginia. The British force was led by General Benedict Arnold, who had been on the side of the Patriots early in the war. On January 4, 1781, Arnold's force arrived at Richmond, Virginia, which had become the capital in 1780. Governor Thomas Jefferson tried to negotiate with Arnold, who offered to spare the capital in exchange for a large

Benedict Arnold served in the Continental army until his identity as a spy for the British was revealed. *(National Archives/DOD, War & Conflict, #62)*

quantity of tobacco that was stored there. When Jefferson refused, Arnold burned much of Richmond. In February, Washington sent the marquis de Lafayette and 1,200 troops to put a stop to Arnold's raids in Virginia.

Washington also dispatched a fleet of French ships and 1,200 French soldiers under the count de Rochambeau to help Lafayette. However, they were met in the Chesapeake on March 16 by an equal British naval force and, after a sea battle, retreated back to their base in Newport, Rhode Island. Arnold continued to cause problems throughout Virginia. He successfully raided the towns of Petersburg, Chesterfield Courthouse, Osborne, and Manchester. He then went back to Petersburg, where he was met by General Lord Cornwallis. Arnold returned to New York, while Cornwallis with a force of 7,500 men planned to finish the job in Virginia.

YORKTOWN

With France now an ally promising to actively participate in the war, Washington thought about attacking British-occupied New York City, the site of his most humiliating defeats early in the war. But after he and the French

Marie-Joseph-Paul-Yves-Roch-Gilbert du Motier, marquis de Lafayette, commanded French troops who joined the colonists in their fight against the British forces. *(National Archives)*

military leader Rochambeau looked over the situation in New York, they decided they did not have the resources to capture the city. They also learned that a French fleet from the Caribbean was headed for Chesapeake Bay. Washington believed that if he could bring all the resources he commanded to bear against Cornwallis, he could end the war in one decisive sweep.

The French fleet arrived in early September 1781 under the command of Admiral François-Joseph-Paul, comte de Grasse. The French fleet had a slight numerical edge but had a huge advantage in firepower over the British fleet that was sent to fight them. During the two-hour battle, the French inflicted so much damage that

François-Joseph-Paul, comte de Grasse, led French forces to aid the colonists during the Battle of Yorktown, thereby helping the colonists win their independence from the British. *(Library of Congress, Prints and Photographs Division [LC-USZ62-45505])*

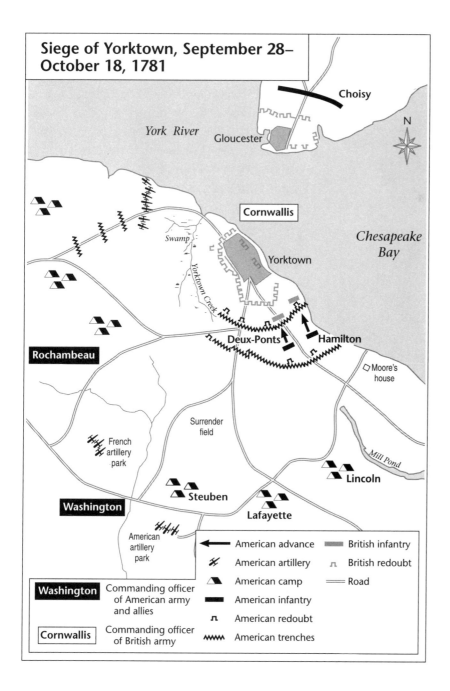

Siege of Yorktown, September 28–October 18, 1781

Choisy

York River

Gloucester

N

Cornwallis

Swamp

Chesapeake Bay

Yorktown

Yorktown Creek

Rochambeau

Deux-Ponts

Hamilton

Moore's house

Surrender field

Mill Pond

French artillery park

Lincoln

Steuben

Washington

Lafayette

American artillery park

←	American advance	▬	British infantry
✗	American artillery	⊓	British redoubt
▲	American camp	══	Road
▬	American infantry		
⊓	American redoubt		
⋀⋀⋀	American trenches		

Washington	Commanding officer of American army and allies
Cornwallis	Commanding officer of British army

the British were forced to retreat to New York. At the same time, a force coming north through the Carolinas fought a battle at Eutaw Springs, South Carolina, on September 8, 1781. Although the British were considered the victors, they suffered such heavy losses that they

Jean-Baptiste-Donatien de Vimeur, comte de Rochambeau, commanded the French army during the Revolutionary War. *(Library of Congress, Prints and Photographs Division [LC-USZ61-158])*

were forced to retreat to Charleston, South Carolina, instead of joining Cornwallis in Virginia.

By the middle of September 1781, Washington, Lafayette, and the French force led by Rochambeau with a combined force of 16,000 troops had Cornwallis trapped at Yorktown, Virginia. De Grasse prevented the British from escaping or receiving help by ship. Part of Washington's strategy was to make the British general Henry Clinton in New York think that was still their objective.

In early October, the combined American/French siege began and the British slowly gave ground. By the middle of the month, Cornwallis knew he had little or no chance of escaping Yorktown. On October 17, 1781, he requested a meeting with his enemies. Terms of surrender were worked out, and on October 19, 1781, General Lord Cornwallis surrendered to George Washington. The war that had started in spring 1775 at the Battle of Lexington and Concord was over, with the victorious George Washington back in his home state of Virginia.

After seven years of fighting, General Cornwallis surrendered at Yorktown on October 17, 1781. *(National Archives)*

9

Building a Nation

After the British had surrendered to George Washington at York-town, it took almost two years for the Treaty of Paris to be signed, officially ending the war. Even after the treaty was signed, on September 3, 1783, it was not until November 25, 1783, that the last British troops left New York City. In Virginia, the Revolution had brought much hardship to the tobacco economy of the state. The last year of war had also caused substantial damage to the towns and plantations that had been raided by British forces led by Benedict Arnold and others.

The situation in the state of Virginia in 1783 looked very similar to the politics of the colony of Virginia that had existed prior the war. Many of the same wealthy planters served in the state government. Those who had died or stepped aside had been replaced by a new generation of privileged landowners, such as George Washington, James Madison, Thomas Jefferson, and George Mason. Washington, Madison, and Jefferson would all later serve as president of the United States. On the surface, it looked like the only real changes were that the royal governor and Crown officials had been replaced by Virginians. However, there were substantial changes to the fabric of Virginia society.

VIRGINIA AFTER THE WAR

One issue that had come up before the Revolution had to do with religion. As in England, the Anglican Church, also called the

The British and the newly independent United States finally compromised when they signed the Treaty of Paris of 1783, two years after the fighting had stopped in the colonies. *(Library of Congress, Prints and Photographs Division [LC-USZ6-279])*

Church of England, was the official church of the colony of Virginia and was supported by taxes. Prior to the war, growing numbers of people had moved into the colony who were not Anglicans. They belonged to Presbyterian, Methodist, Baptist, and other denominations. They objected to supporting churches they did not attend.

The Revolution interrupted the debate about churches as most colonists worked together for independence. However, Mason had included the idea of religious freedom in the Virginia Declaration of Rights when he wrote, ". . . therefore all men are equally entitled to the free exercise of religion, according to the dictates of conscience." To take this one step further, while he was governor in 1779 Thomas Jefferson presented the legislature with a statute for religious freedom. It did not pass at that time. However, after the Revolution, in 1786, Jefferson's friend James Madison reintroduced the bill and it passed, 74 to 20. This bill ended state support of the Anglican Church, which became the Episcopal Church when it separated from the church in England.

The spirit of the American Revolution had affected the thinking of the political leaders of Virginia in more ways than just establishing independence from the Crown. However, for most of the black slaves of Virginia the war changed little.

Slavery was a real dilemma for many of the Patriots in Virginia. Without slavery, they believed they would be unable to return Virginia's fields to profitability. At the same time, they understood that slavery was contradictory to the ideas of freedom many of them had fought for. More than 10,000 slaves were given their freedom by individual planters after the war. Others who considered freeing the slaves did not think there was a place for freed blacks in Virginia society. Thomas Jefferson and others thought that if slaves were freed they should be given their own colony or returned to Africa.

Virginia did pass a law ending the importation of new slaves into the state but would continue to use slaves as the primary source of agricultural and domestic workers through the Civil War. Some Virginians, like Thomas Jefferson, arranged to liberate slaves. Jefferson's slaves were given their freedom after he died.

Some other changes were also seen in Virginia. Jefferson worked to have the law of primogeniture changed. Primogeniture is the rule by which only the oldest son inherits his father's estate. This had been the law in England to help the nobility maintain their estates and hereditary titles. In continuing the lifestyle of the English nobility from whom they descended, the Virginia planters had accepted the rule of primogeniture. In 1786, the legislature passed a law reforming the system of dealing with a family's estate, allowing people to dispose of their property as they saw fit.

One other area where Jefferson worked for reform was in education. Virginia still did not have a system of public education. Jefferson felt that people in all classes of a free society had the ability to learn and achieve. Without public schools, only the wealthy were able to become educated. Jefferson proposed a system of public schools that would make sure that all free Virginians would get at least three years of schooling. His proposal also included additional schooling for any student who showed promise in grammar school. However, the legislature considered Jefferson's plan far too costly for a state that was still suffering economically from the war. It was not until after the Civil War that Virginia opened a public school system.

VIRGINIA AND THE ARTICLES OF CONFEDERATION

In 1776, the Continental Congress asked a committee headed by John Dickinson of Pennsylvania to come up with a plan for the organization of the federal government. The plan that Dickinson submitted to the congress outlined a fairly strong central government. When the debate on the plan started, it quickly became obvious that the states were unwilling to turn power over to a central government. Many delegates were afraid that a strong central government would end up telling the states what to do just as the Crown had.

What the congress was willing to accept was a loose confederation of the states for the purpose of fighting the war. The delegates refused to give the federal government any powers of taxation. The only way the federal government could raise any money was to ask the states for it. The document that came out of this debate is called the Articles of Confederation. Even though it called for a weak central government, it took from 1777 until 1781 to be ratified. The articles required all 13 states to agree, and a few of the smaller states, such as Maryland, Rhode Island, and other states without western land claims, were concerned that the large states such as New York and especially Virginia would come to dominate the country if they were allowed to expand to the west.

In 1781, Virginia and New York gave up their claims in the West to the federal government, and Maryland, the last holdout, ratified the Articles of Confederation. Almost as soon as the articles were put into effect, it became apparent to many that they were inadequate. Without the ability to create taxes, the federal government never had enough money. The states would either ignore requests for funding or send less than was requested. The situation was so desperate that in summer 1783, approximately 100 soldiers

The Bid for the National Capital

One of the issues that faced the United States after the Revolution was where to have the national capital. The First and Second Continental Congresses had met in Philadelphia, but left in 1783 when confronted by the mob of veterans seeking their back pay. The Congress reconvened in Princeton, New Jersey, where it finished its session in 1783.

It was decided at that time that the national capital would alternate between Annapolis, Maryland, and Trenton, New Jersey. The government met in both places, but a permanent home for the capital was still a point of negotiation. Later, New York became the temporary capital. The people of New Jersey wanted the capital permanently, and the New Jersey state legislature offered land and $100,000 to make it happen.

As time went on and the states were working on a new federal constitution, other negotiations were going on. Alexander Hamilton of New York needed the southern states to back his plan to have the federal government assume the debts that the states had incurred during the war. Hamilton sat down with Thomas Jefferson and James Madison and worked out a deal. For their support, Hamilton agreed to see to it that the national capital would be built on the Potomac River in Virginia. Washington, D.C., became the U.S. capital.

The Capitol Building, whose design and construction process was quite complicated, houses the U.S. Senate and House of Representatives. The Capitol dome, visible in this 1859 cross section, was not completed until 1859. The original copper-covered wooden dome was removed in 1856 and replaced with a larger cast-iron dome. *(Architect of the Capitol)*

marched on the hall where the Continental Congress was in session in Philadelphia. These soldiers demanded their back pay. However, the congress had no money. Rather than deal with the soldiers, the Continental Congress was moved to Princeton, New Jersey. Under the Articles of Confederation, the states could not even agree on where the national capital should be.

Other problems also existed under the articles. Each state was able to make its own trade arrangements with foreign merchants. This created competition between the states that caused a number of problems. Representatives from Maryland and Virginia met at Mount Vernon in 1785 and resolved a number of problems regarding shipping in Chesapeake Bay. The Mount Vernon meeting had been so successful that leaders in Virginia suggested that all the states get together in 1786 in Annapolis, Maryland, which was the national capital at the time, to come up with a national plan for the regulation of commerce.

This meeting, known as the Annapolis Convention, took place in early September 1786. Only five states—Virginia, Delaware, New Jersey, New York, and Pennsylvania—sent delegates. Under the Articles of Confederation, it took nine states to agree to anything. The lack of attendance made it impossible for the Annapolis Convention to deal with the trade issues that had brought the states together. However, Alexander Hamilton brought up the inadequacies of the Articles of Confederation. He believed that they were an obstacle to the growth of the nation. Hamilton convinced the delegates at the Annapolis Convention that it was time to make some changes to the articles. The convention issued a report, primarily written by Hamilton, that asked the states to send delegates to a convention in 1787 to review and revise the Articles of Confederation.

James McClurg represented Virginia at the Constitutional Convention. *(Library of Congress, Prints and Photographs Division [LC-USZ62-93489])*

THE CONSTITUTIONAL CONVENTION (1787)

In May 1787, delegates from 12 states (Rhode Island did not send a delegation) came together in Philadelphia, Pennsylvania, for what is now called the Constitutional Convention. The convention elected George

James Madison
(1751–1836)

James Madison was a member of one of Virginia's plantation-owning families and received his early education from a Presbyterian minister named Donald Robertson and the Reverend Thomas Martin. In 1769, the 18-year-old Madison went off to study at the College of New Jersey (later renamed Princeton College), where he earned his degree in 1771. He stayed in Princeton to study law before returning home to Virginia.

In 1774, Madison became a member of the Orange County Committee of Safety, which was in charge of making preparations in case of war with England. In 1776, he was elected to the Virginia State Convention, a meeting of Patriots, where he assisted George Mason in writing the Virginia Declaration of Rights. He is especially given credit for the wording about religious freedom. During this time, he and Thomas Jefferson met and became friends.

After serving in a variety of positions in the revolutionary state government, Madison was elected to the Continental Congress. When the debate over western lands hindered the passage of the Articles of Confederation, it was Madison who was given credit for convincing the political leaders of Virginia and other states to give up their claims to lands in the west. After the war, he returned to Virginia and worked to pass many of the laws recommended by his friend Thomas Jefferson. Madison also advocated giving the federal government the authority to create taxes to pay for its obligations.

At the Constitutional Convention in 1787, James Madison became the primary writer of the Constitution. It is from his notes that historians have been able to understand what went on at the Constitutional Convention. Many of the meetings were closed, and no public records were kept. After the new constitution was completed and sent to the states, Madison joined Alexander Hamilton and John Jay to write 77 essays supporting the acceptance

(continues)

James Madison, a Virginian, earned the nickname "Father of the Constitution" for his contributions to that document. *(Library of Congress, Prints and Photographs Division [LC-USZ62-13004])*

(continued)

of the new constitution. These essays are known as the Federalist Papers, and they helped to turn public opinion in favor of the new constitution.

After the new federal government was in operation, Madison and Jefferson came to disagree with President Washington and his secretary of the treasury, Alexander Hamilton. The disagreement led to the creation of the political party known as the Democratic-Republicans. After Washington's two terms as president, John Adams, who was a member of Washington's Federalist party, became president, and Thomas Jefferson became vice president. When Jefferson became president in 1800, Madison served as his secretary of state. Madison followed Jefferson as president for two terms and then retired to Virginia.

Back in Virginia, Madison once again worked with Jefferson as the two helped to establish the University of Virginia. Madison outlived most of the other "founding fathers." Near the end of his life he wrote, "Having out lived so many of my contemporaries, I ought not to forget that I may be thought to have outlived my self." He died on June 28, 1836, at age 85.

Washington to run the meeting as president. The purpose of the meeting was to review the Articles of Confederation and then make recommendations for changes. However, the convention's delegates quickly saw the futility of trying to fix the Articles of Confederation. Instead, they decided to create an entirely new document. Virginians played a major role in creating the new constitution, and James Madison is credited with being the primary author of the document that came out of the convention.

The Constitution went through numerous debates and compromises before it was ready to be sent to the states for ratification. One of the biggest problems faced by the convention was that of representation in the federal congress. The first plan put forward was called the Virginia Plan. It was introduced by Edmund Randolph but conceived by James Madison. It called for a three-part government made up of the executive, legislative, and judiciary branches. The legislative branch would consist of two houses. One was a lower house, whose representatives would be elected directly by the people on a representational basis, which meant the larger states would have more representatives. The upper house was to be elected by the lower house.

Many of the delegates from smaller states objected to proportional representation in the legislature. They put together an alternative, known as the New Jersey Plan because it was written by one of the delegates from that state. Under the New Jersey Plan, each state would have an equal number of representatives. This plan was unacceptable to the states with larger populations. After three days of debate, the delegates came up with what has been called the Great Compromise. They decided that there would be two houses in the legislature. The House of Representatives would be based on population. The Senate would have two seats for each state.

Another problem that arose was the issue of slaves and slavery. Some northern delegates came from states that had already abolished slavery and wanted the end of slavery to be in the new constitution. Others, mainly from the South, wanted slavery to remain but wanted slaves to count as part of the population of their states. It was finally decided to set aside the question of abolishing slavery until later. For purposes of allotting members of the House of Representatives, a slave was counted as three-fifths of a person.

Edmund Randolph introduced the Virginia Plan to the Constitutional Convention delegates, which called for a government made of legislative, executive, and judiciary branches. *(Library of Congress, Prints and Photographs Division [LC-D416-9861])*

Preamble to the U.S. Constitution

We the People of the United States, in Order to form a more perfect Union, establish Justice, insure domestic Tranquility, provide for the common defence, promote the general Welfare, and secure the Blessings of Liberty to ourselves and our Posterity, do ordain and establish this Constitution for the United States of America.

Once the final document was worked out, it was decided that it would be put into effect when nine states had ratified it. In many states, ratification of the new constitution was not automatic.

RATIFYING THE CONSTITUTION

The delegates from Delaware rushed home at the end of the Constitutional Convention and on December 7, 1787, Delaware became the first state to ratify the new constitution. On June 21, 1788, New Hampshire became the ninth state to ratify the constitution, and the U.S. government as it is known today began. Virginia had yet to ratify, and many in the state had reservations about the new constitution.

Benjamin Harrison, whose son and great-grandson would both be presidents of the United States, was one of the Virginians who had signed the Declaration of Independence. However, he did not support the new constitution. In a letter to George Mason, he wrote, "If the constitution is carried into effect, the states south of the Potomac will be little more than appendages to those northward of it." Patrick Henry and others objected because the constitution did not include a bill of rights.

Promises were made that a bill of rights modeled on the Virginia Declaration of Rights would be added as soon as the new government could get to work. With the Constitution made law by New Hampshire's ratification, debate in Virginia came to an end. Four days after the New Hampshire vote, on June 25, 1788, Virginia ratified the new constitution. It was May 29, 1790, before the final state, Rhode Island, made it unanimous. In December 1791, the first 10 amendments to the constitution, known as the Bill of Rights, were ratified and the United States settled down to try out its new government.

When it came time to elect someone to oversee the new government, there was

After commanding the Continental army throughout the Revolutionary War, George Washington was chosen to be the first president of the United States. *(Library of Congress)*

almost total agreement that George Washington should be the first president of the United States. He took office in 1789 and served two terms. He was followed by John Adams of Massachusetts. Virginia continued to contribute leaders to the new United States as Adams was followed by three Virginians, Thomas Jefferson, James Madison, and James Monroe. Virginia had been one of the centers of the Patriot movement in the colonies, and the contributions it made to the cause of independence were critical. Without the contributions of Virginia, it is hard to imagine that the United States as it is today would have come into being.

Virginia
Time Line

1524

★ Italian Giovanni da Verrazano explores the coast of Virginia for France.

1570

★ Spanish establish a mission on the Rappahannock River.

1606

★ James I grants two companies the right to settle the Atlantic coast of North America.

1607

★ **May:** English settlers land on swampy peninsula on the James River, and establish Jamestown, the first permanent English settlement in North America.

1609

★ London Company issues new charter, which creates a governor.
★ Thomas West, baron De La Warr is appointed governor and heads to Virginia with 500 colonists.

★ **winter:** Without adequate supplies, most of the colonists at Jamestown die of starvation and/or disease. This period is known as the "starving time."

1610

★ **May:** Lord De La Warr arrives with supplies and people to save the colony from being abandoned.

1613

★ John Rolfe develops tobacco that is less bitter than that grown by Native Americans. Tobacco becomes a lucrative cash crop for the colonists.

1614

★ John Rolfe marries Pocahontas, daughter of Powhatan, leader of Powhatan Confederacy, who helps keep peace between Powhatan and settlers.

1618

★ New charter is written, enabling self-government, calling for General Assembly with two chambers, one appointed by the London Company, the Council of State; the other the House of Burgesses, democratically elected.

1619

★ First legislature in Western Hemisphere meets in Jamestown.
★ First slaves arrive in Virginia.
★ Ship arrives with more than 100 women to be brides for male colonists.

1622

★ Opechancanough, Powhatan's brother, attacks white settlements and 350 settlers are killed. Known as the Great Massacre, the incident marks the end of friendly relations between settlers and Native Americans in Virginia.

1624

★ Virginia becomes first royal colony, and the London Company is dissolved; a governor is appointed by the English king.

1629

★ Southern portion of Virginia is given to another proprietor, and Carolina colony is established.

1632

★ Lord Baltimore becomes proprietor of land north of Potomac River, which angers Virginians.

1642

★ Beginning of civil war in England; Virginia remains loyal to king. Many of his supporters, Cavaliers, come to Virginia to seek refuge.

1652

★ The Puritan leader of England, Oliver Cromwell, sends a fleet to Virginia, which forces colony to recognize his government.

1660

★ Charles II becomes king of England, and he refers to Virginia as the "old dominion" for their loyalty. Virginia is still nicknamed the Old Dominion.

1661–76

★ Sir William Berkeley is governor and does not call for elections. This means that a small number of wealthy families stay in power.

1664

★ The Powhatan Confederacy under Opechancanough attacks and kills about 500 colonists. English then force the remaining

Native Americans to move farther west as English settlements expand.

1665

★ Grant created Carolina colony, which encompasses Carolina colony and land south of Currituck Inlet.

1676

★ Bacon's Rebellion—Colonists on frontier wanted protection from rumored Native American attacks; Berkeley refuses; farmers under councilor Nathaniel Bacon organize their own militia.

★ **June:** Bacon's troops burn Jamestown; Bacon dies unexpectedly and rebellion ends.

1700

★ Capital moves from Jamestown to Williamsburg.

1716

★ Governor Alexander Spotswood takes group to Shenandoah Valley over Blue Ridge Mountains and opens the area to settlement.

1747

★ Ohio Company is formed by Tidewater planters to expand westward toward Ohio River over Allegheny Mountains.

1754–63

★ French and Indian War: Virginia is active in the fighting in western Pennsylvania. George Washington gains military experience as commander of the Virginia militia.

1763

★ Treaty of Paris brings an end to conflicts with France.

★ To avoid further trouble with Native Americans, British call for end to westward push beyond Appalachian Mountains but it is not enforced.

1765

★ Virginia House of Burgesses protests Stamp Act and passes the Virginia Resolves.

1765–75

★ Virginia and Massachusetts are the centers of protests against British before Revolution.

1773

★ Patriots form Committee of Correspondence to oversee resistance against the Crown.

1774

★ Governor Dunmore dissolves House of Burgesses although some former burgesses still meet in five state conventions; first convention is called for meeting of all colonies.
★ **May:** Day of prayer is called by House of Burgesses to support Boston whose harbor is closed after Boston Tea Party.
★ **September 5:** First Continental Congress meets in Philadelphia; Peyton Randolph, a Virginia delegate, is elected president.

1775

★ Governor Dunmore seizes powder supply.
★ Militia led by Henry forces Dunmore to pay for powder.
★ Second Continental Congress names George Washington, a Virginia delegate, commander of the newly formed Continental army.
★ **March:** Second Virginia Convention—Burgess Patrick Henry gives his famous speech, calling for action against the British, "Give me Liberty, or give me death!"

1776

★ Patrick Henry is elected first governor.

★ Virginia delegate to Continental Congress Richard Henry Lee introduces motion to Continental Congress for independence from England.

★ Virginia delegate Thomas Jefferson is asked to write Declaration of Independence.

★ **May 15:** Fifth Virginia Convention instructs delegates to Continental Congress to vote for independence from British.

★ **June:** Virginia adopts constitution and declaration of rights, first in colonies.

★ **July 4:** Continental Congress adopts and later signs the Declaration of Independence. Virginians who sign are George Wythe; Richard Henry Lee; Thomas Jefferson; Benjamin Harrison; Thomas Nelson, Jr.; Francis Lightfoot Lee; and Carter Braxton.

1779

★ British take Portsmouth and burn Suffolk.

1780

★ Richmond becomes capital.

1781

★ **January 5:** Benedict Arnold leads British forces to attack and captures Richmond and destroys public buildings.

★ **May:** General Lord Cornwallis, in charge of British forces in America, begins campaign in Virginia.

★ **August:** British fortify Yorktown and Gloucester.

★ **August 21:** George Washington leaves West Point, New York, with 7,000 troops, including French under the comte de Rochambeau, and heads for Virginia.

★ **September 14:** Washington and troops arrive in Williamsburg. French admiral de Grasse has blockaded Chesapeake Bay.

★ **September 28:** Washington and Rochambeau arrive in Yorktown with 16,000 troops.

★ **September 29–October 19:** Siege of Yorktown; American and French ground troops under George Washington and French ships under Admiral de Grasse surround Cornwallis and bombard his troops.

★ **October 17:** Cornwallis asks for truce.

★ **October 19:** Cornwallis surrenders, bringing the American Revolution to a victorious end.

1783

★ **September 3:** Treaty of Paris between the United States and Great Britain is signed.

1787

★ Constitutional Convention convenes in Philadelphia.

★ James Madison is called "Father of the Constitution" because of his work on the Constitution.

1788

★ **June 25:** Virginia Convention ratifies Constitution by 10 votes after a long fight. Virginia becomes the 10th state to ratify the constitution.

Virginia
Historical Sites

ARLINGTON

Ball-Sellers House   The Ball-Sellers House was built by John Ball in the mid-18th century as a one-room log cabin. He later added a lean-to and clapboard siding. The Ball-Sellers House is a rare example of this type of house.

    Address: 5620 Third Street, Arlington, VA 22210
    Phone: 703-379-2123
    Web Site: www.arlingtonhistoricalsociety.org/learn/sites_
       properties/ball-sellers/brief_history.asp

ASHLAND

Slash Christian Church   The Slash Church, built in 1729, is the oldest frame church that survives from colonial times.

    Address: 11353 Mount Hermon Road, Ashland, VA 23005
    Phone: 804-798-4520
    Web Site: www.slashcc.org

BROOKNEAL

Red Hill–Patrick Henry National Monument   Red Hill is the last house Patrick Henry lived in, and it holds his memorabilia.

Address: 1250 Red Hill Road, Brookneal, VA 24528
Phone: 434-376-2044
Web Site: www.redhill.org

CHARLES CITY

Shirley Plantation   Shirley Plantation was established in 1613 and is the oldest plantation in Virginia. Along with the house there are numerous outbuildings, including an old kitchen, stable, and smokehouse.

Address: 501 Shirley Plantation Road, Charles City, VA 23030
Phone: 800-232-1613
Web Site: www.shirleyplantation.com

CHARLOTTESVILLE

Monticello   Monticello was the home of Thomas Jefferson.

Address: 931 Thomas Jefferson Parkway (Virginia Route 53), P.O. Box 316, Charlottesville, VA 22902
Phone: 434-984-9822, recorded information 434-984-9800
Web Site: www.monticello.org

Saturday Morning Walking Tours   The Albemarle Historical Society gives walking tours of historic Charlottesville on Saturdays at 10 A.M. from April through October.

Address: The McIntyre Building, 200 Second Street NE, Charlottesville, VA 22902
Phone: 434-296-1492
Web Site: http://achs.category4.com/Walkingtour/home.html

FREDERICKSBURG

George Washington's Ferry Farm   George Washington lived in this house from age six to 20.

Address: 268 Kings Highway, Fredericksburg, VA 22405
Phone: 540-370-0732
Web Site: www.kenmore.org

GLOUCESTER

Rosewell Ruins   The ruin of Rosewell, one of the most famous colonial houses, which burned in 1916, is open to the public.

Address: 5113 Old Rosewell Lane, Gloucester, VA 23061
Phone: 804-693-2585
Web Site: www.rosewell.org

HOPEWELL

Flowerdew Hundred   Sir George Yeardley first established the plantation Flowerdew Hundred in 1619.

Address: 1617 Flowerdew Hundred Road, Hopewell, VA
23880
Phone: 804-541-8897
Web Site: www.flowerdew.org

LAWRENCEVILLE

Fort Christanna   Fort Christanna was built in 1714 on the banks of the Meherrin River.

Address: Fort Hill Road, Lawrenceville, VA 23868
Phone: 866-783-9768
Web Site: www.tourbrunswick.org/fort_christanna.htm

MASONS NECK

George Mason's Gunston Hall Plantation   Built in about 1755, this is where George Mason lived. The plantation, including a number of outbuildings, has been restored and is open to the public.

Address: 10709 Gunston Road, Masons Neck, VA 22079
Phone: 703-550-9220
Web Site: www.gunstonhall.org

McLean

Claude Moore Colonial Farm   The Claude Moore Colonial Farm depicts life in 1771 on a tenant farm.

Address: 6310 Georgetown Pike, McLean, VA 22101
Phone: 703-442-7557
Web Site: www.1771.org

Mount Vernon

Mount Vernon   Mount Vernon was the home of George Washington. The mansion and numerous outbuildings have been restored and are open to the public.

Address: 3200 George Washington Memorial Parkway, P.O. Box 110, Mount Vernon, VA 22121
Phone: 703-780-2000
Web Site: www.mountvernon.org

Natural Bridge

Monacan Indian Village Complex   Life among the Monacan 300 years ago is portrayed at the Monacan Indian Village Complex.

Address: U.S. 11, Natural Bridge, VA 24578
Phone: 800-533-1410
Web Site: www.naturalbridgeva.com/village.html

Richmond

Wilton House Museum   Wilton House was built for William Randolph III in 1753. Visitors have included George Washington, Thomas Jefferson, and the marquis de Lafayette. It was moved and has been restored and is open to the public.

Address: 215 S. Wilton Road, Richmond, VA 23226
Phone: 804-282-5936
Web Site: www.wiltonhousemuseum.org

WASHINGTON'S BIRTHPLACE

George Washington's Birthplace National Monument George Washington lived here until he was three. The National Park Service has recreated a colonial farm on the site.

> **Address:** 1732 Popes Creek Road, Washington's Birthplace, VA 22443
> **Phone:** 804-224-1732
> **Web Site:** www.nps.gov/gewa

WILLIAMSBURG

Colonial Williamsburg Life in colonial Williamsburg is reenacted amid a number of restored and recreated buildings.

> **Address:** P.O. Box 1776, Williamsburg, VA 23187-1776
> **Phone:** 757-229-1000
> **Web Site:** www.history.org

YORKTOWN

Historic Jamestown The National Park Service Center houses a museum of 17th-century materials. In addition, tours of the Jamestown site are available.

> **Address:** Colonial National Historical Park, P.O. Box 210, Yorktown, VA 23690
> **Phone:** 757-229-1733
> **Web Site:** www.nps.gov/colo

Further Reading

BOOKS

Billings, Warren M., John E. Selby, and Thad W. Tate. *Colonial Virginia: A History.* White Plains, N.Y.: KTO Press, 1986.

Britton, Tamara L. *The Virginia Colony.* Edina, Minn.: ABDO, 2001.

Bruchac, Joseph. *Pocahontas.* Orlando, Fla.: Silver Whistle, 2003.

Da Capua, Sarah. *The Virginia Colony.* Chanhassen, Minn.: Child's World, 2004.

Fradin, Dennis B. *Virginia Colony.* Chicago: Children's Press, 1986.

Hossel, Karen Price. *Virginia.* San Diego, Calif.: Lucent, 2002.

WEB SITES

Association for the Preservation of Virginia Antiquities. "History of Jamestown." Available online. URL: http://www.apva.org/history/index.html. Downloaded on August 2, 2004.

Colonial Williamsburg. "Explore & Learn." Available online. URL: www.history.org/Almanack/life/life.cfm. Downloaded on August 6, 2004.

Virginia Historical Society. "The Story of Virginia." Available online. URL: http://www.vahistorical.org/storyofvirginia.htm. Downloaded on August 5, 2004.

Index

Page numbers in *italic* indicate photographs. Page numbers in **boldface** indicate box features. Page numbers followed by m indicate maps. Page numbers followed by c indicate time line entries. Page numbers followed by t indicate tables or graphs.

public school system 102
Puritans 42, 112c
    and Cavaliers 42
    and civil war 41
    colony of 13
    defeat of 45, **46**
    rule of 42–44

Q

Quakers 67, 90
quartering of troops 80
Queen Anne's War 60, 62, **62**

R

raids
    by colonists 38, 39, 48
    by Loyalists 87
    by Native Americans 48–50
    on plantations 55, 88
Raleigh, Sir Walter 2, 3
Randolph, Edmund 106, 107
Randolph, Peyton 80, 114c
Ratcliffe, John 20, 24
ratification 106, 108–109, 116c
Rebecca **25**
recession 60
Red Hill–Patrick Henry National
    Monument 117–118
Reformation, Protestant viii
regional struggle 48
religion 99–101. *See also specific head-*
    ings, e.g.: Catholicism and Catholics
religious dissent viii, ix
religious freedom
    debate over 100, 101
    and James Madison **105**
Renaissance viii
representation
    in Congress 106–107
    no taxation without 76, 77
    proportional 107
    and slavery 107
Revere, Paul 78
Revolutionary War. *See American Rev-*
    olution
Rhode Island xiim, 108
rice 46
Richmond, Virginia 44, 94–95, 115c
Roanoke colony 2–3, 4

Roanoke Indians 4
Roanoke Island 2, 4
Rochambeau, count de (Jean-Bap-
    tiste-Donatien de Vimeur) 95, 98,
    97m, 115c
Rolfe, John
    and Pocahontas **25,** 32, 111c
    and tobacco 29, 111c
Rolfe, Thomas **25**
Rosewell Ruins 119
royal charters x, **59**
royal colony 40, 112c

S

St. Augustine, Florida 2
saplings (in house building) 9, 10
Saratoga, New York 94
Saturday Morning Walking Tours of
    Charlottesville 118
Savannah, Georgia 94
Scotland **14**
Second Continental Congress. *See*
    Continental Congress, Second
Senate, U.S. 103, 107
settlement(s). *See also* colonization
    English 13–26, 110c
    first 13–26
    Jamestown colony 13–14,
        20–21. *See also* Jamestown
        colony
    in the Piedmont 58, 63
    Plymouth colony 13
    in Shenandoah Valley 58
    Spanish 2, 110c
    by Vikings vii
shallop 20
shellfish 8
Shenandoah Valley
    settlement in 58
    and Spotswood expedition 63,
        64, 113c
    surveying of 64
shipping and ships
    attacks on 60
    English 44, 46
    galleons ix, x
    of tobacco 60, 60
    treasure 2
    Viking viii

shipwreck 28
Shirley Plantation 118
sinew 8
Siouan-speaking Indians 3, 5m,
    39
Slash Christian Church 117
slaves/slavery **57**
    abolition of 107
    and Constitution (U.S.) 107
    curing tobacco 29
    and the Dutch 34
    first arrival of 34, 111c
    freeing of 87, 88, 101
    importation of 101
    increase in 62
    and indentured servants **16,**
        34
    at Jamestown 33
    as labor source 34
    and plantation system 34
    in population 57, 58
    and representation 107
    runaway 88
    of John Smith **18, 19**
    in Tidewater 58
    and tobacco growing 30, 31
    uprising of 87, 88
    and war for independence 101
sloop 20
smallpox 11, 12, 12
Smith, John x, 17, **18,** 50
    accounts of 10, 11, 23, 24
    arrest of 19
    capture of **18, 19,** 23, 24, **25,**
        25–26
    as governor 26
    and London Company **19**
    and Native Americans 24, 27
    and Opechancanough 38
    and Pocahontas 24, 25, **25,** 26
    and Powhatan Indians 23, 24,
        24–26, **25,** 38
    trading of 24, 25, 27
    and Edward Marie Wingfield 19,
        20
    writings of 18, **19,** 26
smoking of tobacco **30**
smuggling 47, 79
social divisions 47, 48

Virginia (continued)
land claims of 102, **105**
map of 43m
naming of 2
population in 12, 34, 57, 58, 58t
and ratification 108, 116c
Virginia Company of London. See
London Company
Virginia Company of Plymouth 13
Virginia Convention, First 80
Virginia Convention, Second 82, 83,
114c
Virginia Declaration of Rights 115c
and Bill of Rights 88, **89,** 108
and Declaration of Independence
88, **89**
and James Madison **105**
and religious freedom 100–101
Virginia Plan 107
Virginia Resolves **75,** 76, 114c
Virginia State Convention **89**
voting rights **54**

W

Wahunsonakok. See Powhatan (chief)
war. See also specific heading, e.g.: French
and Indian War
confederation for fighting 102
and Patrick Henry 80
warfare
European style 68
intertribal 8
and Native Americans 11, **39**

War of Independence. See American
Revolution
Washington, D.C. **103**
Washington, George
and Benedict Arnold 95
at Constitutional Convention
104, 106
defeats of 93
and First Continental Congress 80
as first president 108, 109
and French and Indian War
65–68, 84, 113c
as general 84–86, 86, 93–95,
97m, 98, 114c
historic sites for 118–121
and James Madison **106**
and Ohio Company 64
as privileged landowner 99
surrender of 66
surveys Shenandoah Valley 64
at Valley Forge 93, 94
victories of 94
at Battle of Yorktown 95, 97m,
98, 115c, 116c
Washington, John 49
water (drinking) 21
wealth
concentration of 62
search for 16
wealthy families 112c
the West 102, **105**
West, Thomas. See De La Warr, 12th
baron 27, 28, 110c, 111c

West Virginia 63
westward expansion 63–64
White, John 4
wigwams 9, 10
Wilderness, Battle of the 68
William and Mary, College of. See College of William and Mary
Williamsburg, Virginia
as capital 58, 113c
colonial 121
Lord Dunmore flees from 87
Wilton House Museum 120–121
Wingfield, Edward Maria 19–20,
24
women
brides 33–34, 111c
as colonists 26, 33–34, 111c
farming by 6
at Jamestown colony 26
Pocahontas 24, 25, **25,** 26, 32,
111c
Woodford, William 88
Woodland Culture 4, 5
and family 10
housing of 9, 9, 10
wooly mammoth 3
Wren, Sir Christopher **59,** 59
Wythe, George 93, 115c

Y

Yeardley, Sir George 33, 35
Yorktown, Battle of 95, 96, 97m, 98,
98, 99, 115c–116c